THE
ROADMAP
TO HOSPITAL CARE

INSIGHTS ON PREPARING FOR HEALTH EMERGENCIES
& HOSPITAL STAYS WITH CONFIDENCE

SHADI VAHDAT, MD

For more information, email shadivahdatmd@gmail.com.

ISBN: 979-8-89109-870-1 - paperback
ISBN: 979-8-89109-871-8 - ebook
ISBN: 979-8-89109-872-5 - hardcover

GET YOUR FREE GIFT!

Discover invaluable insights and expert advice in the book *The Roadmap To Hospital Care: Insights on Preparing for Health Emergencies and Hospital Stays with Confidence.*

To enhance your learning, we're offering FREE Action Item Lists and Essential Guides. These resources distill the book's key takeaways into easy-to-access tools.

Make sure to DOWNLOAD your FREE resources by visiting: www.shadivahdatmd.com/freeresources

BONUS RESOURCE:
DR. VAHDAT'S INSIGHTFUL TED TALK

For an inspiring real-life example of health advocacy, explore Dr. Vahdat's TED talk, "Can We Change How We Respond to Bad News." This talk delves into a personal journey of advocating for a misdiagnosed cancer case, highlighting the power of second opinions and the importance of staying composed amid alarming medical news. It's a perfect complement to the themes explored in *The Roadmap To Hospital Care*.

Access the talk by visiting: https://www.youtube.com/watch?v=otfBGA2r3lw

This book is dedicated to my Baba, in whose memory I found the strength and inspiration to write this book.

TABLE OF CONTENTS

INTRODUCTION

I clearly remember the night, a week before he would be gone from our lives forever, when Dad got admitted to the hospital. Less than forty-eight hours earlier, I'd been frantically driving around Los Angeles looking for the best nursing home so he could recover from his pelvic fracture. An unexpected call changed all that.

Earlier in the day, he'd called me, panicking, to say he had a sudden, bad stomachache. He didn't feel well, he explained, and the paramedics were coming to take him to the hospital for further evaluation.

I was worried, but this wasn't a new feeling. Over the course of my life, I'd gotten many frantic calls from him. His heart had given up years before, when he was diagnosed with heart failure, and little by little, the rest of his organs followed. He suffered from more heart attacks than I could remember. Slowly, his kidneys failed to the point of dialysis. Next his liver failed, requiring the drainage of the fluid in his belly on a monthly basis. Seeing the strongest and toughest person I knew wither away to nothing more than skin and bones, constantly in excruciating pain and discomfort, was more than I could handle. It was slow torture.

I'd been worried about losing my father for as long as I can remember. He suffered his first heart attack before I turned ten; from then on, I was always scared something terrible was going to take him away from me. When I was in high school, my parents separated, and my worries for him continued to escalate because I no longer lived with him. After the divorce, my concerns for him included his mental health as well. In college, he came to live with me briefly, and I periodically needed to interrupt my studying to take him to the emergency room—typically for another episode of chest pain. On one of those evenings, in a hospital in Oakland, California, there were what looked like bloodstains on the curtain dividing our space from the next patient. It was all terrifying, and at that young age, I felt helpless and confused, not knowing how to help him.

A few years after the divorce, Dad decided to return to the Middle East, which meant I had a more distant role in his medical ups and downs. He ultimately married his nurse from one of his hospitalizations and restarted his life across the globe with his new family. Meanwhile, I was attending medical school and gaining my own experience as a hospital doctor. Even when we were a world apart, I don't recall a time when I wasn't worried about his health. I heard about his repeated heart attacks, an eventual bypass and its complications, and multiple cardiac arrests. Once, he was pronounced dead when he didn't immediately respond to resuscitation efforts. The medical drama he endured seemed never-ending. But, like the bionic man, he somehow managed to survive and keep going.

Ten years before his eventual passing, he called to say the doctors were essentially done with him. There was nothing else they could do. His medical problems had become too complex for their medical system. His doctors thought his safest option was to travel to the US for the lifesaving medical treatments and procedures he needed. This was when I became more engaged in his care, trying to get him the help he needed. For a period of time, I even managed his medications and took care of him from across the world because I knew no other doctor wanted to take that responsibility. I got the details of his medical files, labs, and images, then discussed them with my physician friends and colleagues. I was determined to do whatever it took to give him a fighting chance.

When he finally moved back to the US, I took him to the best heart doctor in my hospital, and he received his pacemaker. With carefully selected doctors and facilities— and a heavy-handed dose of patient advocacy—we were able to prolong Dad's life for nearly a decade longer. Those years, especially the last three, weren't easy. He required monthly hospitalizations and dialysis, and he experienced slow deterioration of nearly every organ.

While Dad had a long list of medical problems that could fill multiple pages, he didn't take the necessary steps that would ease his (and my) pain and suffering in his last days.

My initial intention for writing the book was to build greater awareness around the myriad of challenges that anyone may encounter if hospitalized. Following my dad's passing, my primary goal was to shed light on what went wrong and how we could have helped him transition from this life with more comfort and dignity. Back then, all I could think about were the unfortunate events that led up to him being admitted to a hospital that would never be my first choice.

With time, I've gained a broader view of everything that led us to that unfortunate last week. I have often wondered how things could have gone differently for a more peaceful ending. In Chapters 1 through 3, I'll explain the steps and strategies you should think about before any hospital visit becomes necessary—even if you don't anticipate needing one anytime soon. In Chapter 4, I'll focus on steps and strategies during an acute illness, which may prevent a hospitalization or lead to a brief emergency room stay. Chapter 5 to the end of the book covers the course of events after hospital admission to final discharge (and everything in between). This book is designed to be a helpful companion, guide, and reference, no matter your current situation. You don't have to read it cover to cover; think of it more like a reference book you can turn to as needed.

The difficult process of reliving every painful moment to write this book has made the value of advance planning very clear to me. Thinking ahead surely lessens the burden of critical decision-making during tough times. Nevertheless, despite our best preparations, difficult days may still arise in any health journey.

It's important to recognize that, despite your best efforts, certain aspects of health will always remain beyond your control. During these trying times, remember that educating yourself, preparing, and planning, even to a small extent, can be empowering. Embracing hope when uncertainty looms and staying grounded can lead to more positive outcomes. It's also important to know when to let go without harboring guilt or regret, as this can provide immeasurable comfort. I hope the guidance in this book will leave you with a sense that you've taken major steps to prepare for medical uncertainties. Regardless of the outcome, even in the face of loss, may you find victory in knowing you've advocated fiercely for yourself or a loved one.

As a hospital physician with over two decades of experience in some of the nation's top medical institutions, I've seen healthcare from both sides. I've seen my colleagues face tough challenges, working tirelessly to provide excellent care. I've also been a caregiver, daughter, wife, and mother dealing with life-threatening illnesses in my own family.

This book isn't about dwelling on the hardships or obstacles; it is a guiding light that illuminates the path ahead. I invite you to go on the journey with me, exploring the insights and experiences I've gathered. Together, we can navigate the maze of healthcare, making choices that resonate best with your unique health goals and values.

If you're ready to prepare and educate yourself, turn the page.

CHAPTER 1

KNOW YOUR HOSPITALS

I think about the amount of time and effort some of us put into looking at *Consumer Reports* to buy the safest car, the best washing machine, or the newest electronic device. Yet how many of us research hospitals or medical facilities that we'll use in our time of greatest need? While we would like to think all hospitals provide the same quality of care, the reality is much different. Unfortunately, my family learned this the hard way.

A few years before my dad passed, he was looking to move to a new home. By this point, we'd established his care with a great team of doctors at a teaching hospital. This meant he got care from a highly specialized team of doctors who were experts in their respective fields, including:

- A cardiologist who specialized in heart failure
- An electrophysiologist who specialized in irregular heart rhythms and pacemakers
- A nephrologist, or kidney doctor, for a failing kidney and dialysis
- A hepatologist, or liver specialist, for a failing liver
- A hematologist, or blood doctor, for abnormal bleeding

- A gastroenterologist for chronic abdominal pain and life-threatening infections
- An ear-nose-throat doctor for sinus congestion and nosebleeds
- An ophthalmologist, or eye doctor, for constant, painful eye complaints
- An extensivist, who specialized in bridging his care between hospitalizations and outpatient care

Surely, a highly specialized medical center would be one of the best places to deliver the care that such a complex and ill patient needed. Yet, when my dad was deciding where to live, the value and importance of ease and accessibility to such a center were overlooked.

Despite my strong recommendation that he live close to the doctors who knew him so well, he decided to move nearly an hour away (which, with Los Angeles traffic, ended up being closer to two hours). A trip to see any of these doctors was nearly an all-day event. First, he needed to call the transportation service two days in advance for pickup. He typically had to leave home several hours in advance since the car service needed extra time for picking up other passengers on the way to the clinic. He spent thirty to sixty minutes waiting for the doctor, and another thirty to sixty minutes for labs, tests, or procedures. The transportation pickup for the trip back home was often a more unpredictable affair. Many times, the car service failed to show up, leaving us to arrange the ride home ourselves. He typically got back late in the afternoon or even after dark, extremely fatigued, turning his trip to the second-floor bedroom into a dangerous journey.

Having a two-story home without a downstairs bedroom was another issue he—like most people—didn't consider. This one issue by itself came with grave consequences, as frailty, disability, balance, and mobility issues worsened.

Even disregarding the inconvenience of routine clinic visits, the profound impact of living far away from his home medical center, where his doctors knew him best, became glaringly evident during his last week of life. Paramedics transferred him from his rehabilitation facility to the nearest hospital. However, the closest hospital lacked the specialized medical staff and advanced resources available at the hospital where his own trusted doctors practiced. Even more critical, it lacked access to his medical records, a setback that would be a challenge for any patient but was particularly concerning for someone with such a complex history.

He was admitted in the middle of the night—confused and lethargic—and taken care of by a completely new set of doctors unfamiliar with his case. This was the start of a very scary situation that got worse day by day. It was particularly frustrating for me because I knew the care he would get at this hospital was far below the standard I was used to. The number of staff and attention given to patients, the level of expertise, the equipment and machines used—everything paled in comparison to what I was used to. I knew things weren't ideal but hoped for the best and set a goal to get him transferred as soon and as safely as possible.

The importance of proximity to Dad's medical home played such an important role in the last week of his life that I must mention it early in this book. We would have achieved a much better outcome if more research had been done before the crisis. While living close to a highly specialized hospital may not be realistic for many, it can be very helpful, if not essential, to plan ahead and compare local facilities, especially for those with advancing age or complex medical issues. In my dad's case, choosing a closer rehab facility connected to his own medical center could have been one option. Or we could have connected with local primary care providers affiliated with his local hospital, who could have taken a more active role when he was hospitalized.

In Chapter 2, I delve deeper into the process of finding a team of providers who will be the best fit for you. However, as this book primarily centers around hospital stays, I'll begin by providing insights into the specific type of hospital you may find yourself in.

You may think it's better to find a good heart or lung doctor and just go to whatever hospital they're affiliated with. But in my experience (which includes experiencing the inner workings of several hospitals in greater Los Angeles County), the hospital staff matter more when it comes to a hospital stay. During most hospitalizations, and particularly in the first few hours or days, you're most likely going to be in the hands of a team of hospital doctors. If you're admitted in the middle of the night or on a weekend, chances are the hospital staff caring for you won't even be able to reach your primary care doctor or specialist. This means they may or may not have access to your medical history when they evaluate you. So, to ensure high-quality care, you need to research the hospitals near your home and choose one that ranks high across the board.

Luckily, in Los Angeles, my family and I are conveniently located an equal distance from two or three excellent medical centers. I've had enough experience to know which hospital I would prefer in an emergency, and which would be my second choice. Unfortunately, we haven't always been able to align our favorite hospital with our favorite private doctors. My family does a bit of picking and choosing—we visit one health facility for some specialties, and we go to a different location for others. Wouldn't it be ideal to find excellent specialists or primary doctors who are affiliated with the best hospital in town? Surely that would be ideal, but it's not always possible.

When it comes to choosing a hospital, the ideal scenario involves having a trusted primary care doctor affiliated with an outstanding hospital that's part of a broader network of medical professionals *and* knowing they're willing to get involved with your care if you require hospitalization. You don't need to ensure your primary care provider is physically going to care for you at the hospital, but it would be good to know they're at least willing to communicate your history, needs, and goals to those taking care of you during a hospitalization. Having a primary care doctor who knows you well and is willing to advocate for you is priceless! When you're generally healthy and haven't required hospitalizations, your focus should be on researching and finding the best primary care options while also exploring local medical facilities. The ultimate goal is to find a practical, accessible, and trustworthy pairing of both, ensuring your healthcare needs are well supported.

DIFFERENT TYPES OF HOSPITALS

Hospitals come in all shapes and sizes, and there are about 6,093 of them in the US.[1] It's important to look into the differences between these hospitals because some might be better fits for your healthcare needs. Let's break down these differences in more detail.

NONPROFIT VERSUS FOR-PROFIT HOSPITALS

While there are supposed to be some major differences between these two types of hospitals, it's important to recognize that the patient experience may differ quite a bit depending on the hospital in question. For instance, you might assume that nonprofits are more focused on community well-being and may offer lower-cost care. In contrast, for-profits may be seen as primarily profit-driven, potentially leading to higher costs and less emphasis on patient satisfaction. However, it's crucial to understand that these stereotypes don't always hold true because each hospital is unique and has its own mission, values, and practices. To make an informed decision about your healthcare, it's essential to look beyond the stereotypes, do your research, and consider the factors that matter most to you. Let's dive into some differences below.

NONPROFIT HOSPITALS

1. **Patient-Centric:** They prioritize patient outcomes and satisfaction.
2. **Tax Exemptions:** Reported to benefit from more than $24 billion in federal, state, and local tax exemptions each year.[2]
3. **Community Obligations:** In return for financial benefits, they must provide research, charity care, improved community health, and education, regardless of a patient's financial status[3]

4. **Community Responsiveness:** They must provide a faster response to community needs, such as during pandemics.
5. **Specialized Services:** They offer specialized services like neonatal care, trauma and burn centers.

POTENTIAL CONCERNS

1. **Tax Benefits versus Charity:** There may be some discrepancies between the tax breaks a hospital receives and the charitable work it does in return for those breaks. Concerns can be either an actual discrepancy or a lack of transparency regarding definitions of charitable obligations.[4]
2. **Executive Salaries:** There are concerns regarding high executive salaries in some large nonprofit medical systems.[5]
3. **Financial Instability:** Rising labor costs and inflation-related pressures potentially lead to more mergers and acquisitions.[6]
4. **Billing Bureaucracy:** Patients may face administrative hurdles and confusion when dealing with billing issues.
5. **Longer Wait Times:** Some nonprofit hospitals have extended wait times for care, especially in emergency rooms.
6. **Relocation to Wealthier Areas:** Criticism has developed as some nonprofit hospitals move from lower-income to wealthier areas, potentially neglecting underserved populations.[7]

FOR-PROFIT HOSPITALS

1. **Profit-Focused:** These hospitals are owned by investors with a responsibility to their shareholders.
2. **Access to Advanced Technology**: For-profit hospitals often invest in the latest medical equipment and

technology to attract patients and provide cutting-edge treatments.

3. **Convenience**: Due to their competitive nature, for-profit hospitals may offer more convenient scheduling and shorter wait times for appointments and procedures.

4. **Patient Experience**: The profit motive can drive for-profit hospitals to focus on delivering high-quality care to attract and retain patients, potentially leading to a better patient experience.

5. **Innovation in Services**: The drive for profitability can encourage for-profit hospitals to offer innovative services, such as specialized wellness programs, health screenings, and outpatient services, which can benefit patients.

POTENTIAL CONCERNS[8]

1. **Cost Concerns**: For-profit hospitals may have more inflated fees, with potential for higher costs for uninsured, low-income, and out-of-network patients.

2. **Profit over Patients**: Critics raise concerns for prioritization of profits over patient care.

For-profit hospitals, as businesses, aim to generate profits, and this can sometimes lead to cost-cutting measures or decisions that prioritize financial gains. In some cases, this could potentially impact patient care.

3. **Community Commitment**: They have a lower commitment to community and charitable services.

4. **Limited Access**: For-profits have the potential to provide limited care to those who can't pay.

While these are some general points to consider, it's important to note that some nonprofit hospitals may be more expensive than for-profit hospitals, and some for-profit hospitals may be more likely to accept and care for patients with limited financial resources or government-funded health insurance. So, it's worth spending some time comparing your options before making a decision.

TEACHING OR NONTEACHING HOSPITAL

I've worked in both types of facilities for the last twenty-five years, with the last fifteen exclusively at a teaching hospital. I firmly believe that whether you're choosing a hospital, doctor, or any healthcare provider, it's crucial that you understand their offerings, expertise, and limitations. Planning ahead to gain this knowledge can help you make better-informed healthcare decisions and minimize future frustrations, even though emergencies don't always allow for such choices. Out of all the hospitals in the US, only about 5% are considered teaching hospitals, yet they play a major role by offering 98% of the nation's comprehensive cancer centers, 69% of the total burn unit beds, 63% of pediatric intensive care unit beds, and 24% of inpatient psychiatric beds. Additionally, these hospitals serve a disproportionately large number of Medicare and Medicaid beneficiaries, as well as individuals without insurance.[9] Let's look at some differences below:

TEACHING HOSPITALS
PROS

1. **Access to Advanced Care**: They have high-quality resources and up-to-date treatment options.
2. **Optimal Expertise**: Medical staff at teaching hospitals undergo extensive hands-on training, providing a higher level of expertise in a wide range of medical cases.
3. **Cutting-Edge Research**: They're at the forefront of medical research. Patients may have opportunities

to participate in clinical trials and gain access to experimental treatments and procedures.

4. **Specialized Care**: They're more likely to have specialized departments and centers, such as for cancer or neurosurgery, making them equipped to handle complex and rare medical conditions.

5. **Collaborative Care**: They typically have teams of specialists from various healthcare disciplines working together to provide well-rounded patient care. This multidisciplinary approach ensures that all aspects of a patient's health are considered and addressed effectively.

6. **Survival Rates**: Major teaching hospital status was associated with lower mortality rates, in comparison to nonteaching hospitals, but this area requires more investigation to draw definitive conclusions.[10]

CONS

1. **Longer Wait Times**: Due to the teaching structure, patients may experience longer wait times and more involvement from more junior or inexperienced trainees, which can be frustrating for some.

2. **Overnight Care**: Admissions during the night may involve care from junior doctors due to fewer senior doctors on duty, potentially affecting the level of care.

3. **Higher Costs**: They may be more expensive than nonteaching hospitals because of their academic programs and research, potentially leading to higher healthcare bills.

4. **Inconsistent Care**: The quality of care between hospitals and even providers in the same hospital can vary, as it depends on the length of training and experience of the junior doctors and the quality of supervision from more senior doctors.

NONTEACHING HOSPITALS
PROS

1. **Efficiency**: They often provide more streamlined care, with fewer layers of doctors and trainees involved, which often leads to quicker service.
2. **Lower Costs**: They tend to have lower overhead costs, which may result in more affordable healthcare.
3. **Patient Experience**: Patients may feel these hospitals provide a more personalized experience.
4. **Experienced Staff**: Only attending physicians, who have completed their training, manage patients. This can be reassuring for patients.
5. **Focus on Primary Care**: They may provide more access to primary care services, making them suitable for routine healthcare needs.

CONS

1. **Limited Specialized Care**: Nonteaching hospitals are more likely to have general specialists treating a variety of conditions, while teaching hospitals have teams of highly specialized doctors, including general gastroenterologists, hepatologists (liver specialists), or even inflammatory bowel specialists. This could translate into them being less equipped to handle complex or rare medical conditions.
2. **Limited Research**: They may not engage in as much cutting-edge research, potentially limiting access to the latest treatments and clinical trials.
3. **Outdated Technology**: Some nonteaching hospitals may be behind in adopting the latest medical technologies and treatment methods.

The choice between teaching and nonteaching hospitals depends on various factors, including your specific medical needs and preferences, as well as the availability of different healthcare facilities in your region.

LOCATION: RURAL AND URBAN

The classification of hospitals as rural or urban varies significantly from state to state. Rural hospitals are typically found in less densely populated areas, while urban hospitals are situated in more populated regions. In some states, like Idaho, Montana, and South Dakota, more than 90% of hospitals are classified as rural,[11] reflecting their less densely populated areas. In contrast, Washington DC, New Jersey, and Rhode Island have very few rural hospitals. It's possible to find both nonprofit and for-profit hospitals in both rural and urban settings, yet teaching hospitals are generally more likely to be found in urban areas. There are exceptions, as some rural regions have smaller teaching hospitals or medical school satellite campuses to address community healthcare needs and provide medical education in less populated areas.

RURAL HOSPITALS
PROS

1. **Comprehensive Services**: Small rural hospitals differ from urban hospitals by not only offering traditional services like emergency care, inpatient care, and laboratory testing but also by providing rehabilitation, long-term care, and primary care.[12]
2. **Lower Cost of Services**: Rural areas often have lower operating costs, which can lead to more affordable healthcare services. In some cases, charges in rural hospitals can be up to 56% lower than urban hospitals.[13]

3. **Shorter Wait Times**: They may have shorter wait times for emergency care and elective procedures due to lower patient volumes.[14]

CONS

1. **Limited Resources**: They tend to have fewer resources, including specialized medical equipment and healthcare professionals, which can limit services provided.

2. **Limited Specialists**: Access to specialists can be difficult in rural areas, making it harder on patients with more complex conditions. Rural communities have only 6% of the nation's OB/GYNs (obstetrics/gynecologists).[15]

3. **Staff Shortages**: Recruiting and retaining physicians can be difficult in rural areas, leading to a higher likelihood of getting care by midlevel providers, like physician assistants or nurse practitioners.

4. **Financial Challenges**: They may struggle financially due to lower patient volumes and higher rates of uncompensated care. A report from the American Hospital Association notes that a record 19 facilities were closed in 2020 alone due to low reimbursement, staffing shortages, financial challenges from the COVID-19 pandemic, and other increasing expenses.[16]

5. **Mortality Rates**: In 2019, rural areas experienced higher mortality rates for the top 10 causes of death compared to their urban counterparts. The most significant disparities were observed in mortality rates attributed to heart disease, cancer, and chronic lower respiratory disease.[17] In all likelihood, the public health challenges and strains brought on by the pandemic have only worsened the existing differences.

URBAN HOSPITALS
PROS

1. **Advanced Services**: They often offer a wider range of specialized medical services and have access to cutting-edge technology and research.
2. **Specialist Availability**: Urban areas typically have a higher concentration of healthcare specialists.
3. **Teaching and Research Opportunities**: Many urban hospitals are affiliated with medical schools, offering opportunities for medical education and participation in research.
4. **Diverse Patient Populations**: They serve diverse patient populations, providing exposure to a wide range of medical conditions.

CONS

1. **High Patient Volume**: They can be very busy, leading to longer wait times and crowded facilities.
2. **Complex Bureaucracy**: Larger urban hospitals have more complex administrative structures, which can create challenges in decision-making and communication.
3. **Health Disparities**: While urban hospitals have access to advanced care, they may also face challenges related to health disparities, including issues of access for underserved populations.

The pros and cons of rural and urban hospitals can vary depending on the specific location, the needs of the population they serve, and the resources available to them. You should consider these factors when making decisions about where to receive medical care.

HOSPITAL SIZE AND BED CAPACITY

Hospital size and bed capacity of healthcare facilities have proven to be critical factors during any significant pandemic or surge in specific illness. The fear and uncertainty of having a family member with a severe illness requiring an intensive care unit bed and the inability to secure one can be a daunting experience.

Hospitals vary in size and capacity, and they can be classified into different categories based on their sizes and the ranges of services they offer. Here are some common categories of hospitals based on size:

1. **Small Community Hospitals**
    *   They're typically smaller and serve rural or small communities.
    *   They may have fewer than 100 beds.
    *   They provide basic medical services, such as emergency care, general surgery, and primary care.
2. **Medium-Sized Community Hospitals**
    *   They have between 100 and 250 beds.
    *   They offer a wider range of services, including specialty care in areas like obstetrics, pediatrics, and orthopedics.
3. **Large Community Hospitals**
    *   They're bigger and more comprehensive in terms of services.
    *   They typically have between 250 and 500 beds.
    *   They may have more specialized departments, including intensive care units (ICUs), cardiology, and imaging services.

4. **Teaching Hospitals (Academic Medical Centers)**
   - They're associated with medical schools and universities.
   - They can vary in size but often have over 500 beds.
   - They focus on medical education and research in addition to patient care.
   - They provide a wide range of specialized services and are often equipped with advanced technology.
5. **Specialty Hospitals**
   - They focus on specific medical areas, such as orthopedics, cancer treatment, or cardiac care.
   - Size can vary widely depending on specialization.
6. **Children's Hospitals**
   - They specialize in pediatric care and are dedicated to treating children and adolescents.
   - They come in various sizes, from small, specialty hospitals to large, comprehensive children's medical centers.

It's important to note that hospital size can vary not only in terms of the number of beds but also in the services offered, patient populations served, and level of medical expertise available.

KNOW YOUR HOSPITAL OPTIONS

Whether you have the luxury of choosing your medical center or are limited to the only option available for miles, understanding your options is crucial when it comes to healthcare. This understanding includes being aware of the potential risks associated with medical care, particularly concerning medical errors, which is a topic of hot debate. Estimates of annual deaths attributed to hospital errors vary widely, from the 98,000 deaths reported by the Institute of Medicine based on its 1984 data review to more recent estimates of 440,000 deaths from late 2000s data.[18] These deaths can be linked to infections, errors, injuries, and accidents that may occur during a hospital stay. While those numbers are frightening on their own, they don't even account for all the cases of injury or harm that don't result in death! Therefore, researching your hospital options and being informed about the potential risks can be critical.

It's commonly known that there may be several causes for the underreporting of medical errors. Healthcare mistakes may not always get reported because healthcare workers worry about what might happen if they speak up. They might fear getting in trouble, being blamed for the mistake, or facing legal action. Some workplaces have cultures that tend to blame individuals instead of looking at the bigger picture, making people hesitant to report errors. There's also a concern that staff might face negative consequences or backlash from their colleagues or bosses for speaking up.

STARTING YOUR RESEARCH

You might be wondering how you would even start your research on your local facilities. While you may need to look at different resources to get information for your local hospital, the research will be well worth it. The easiest place to start may be getting the opinions of your trusted doctors and specialists. Then I suggest doing a bit of detective work on your own and looking at multiple sources. Next, don't forget that friends' and family members' experiences with a medical center can be incredibly informative. Combining and evaluating all these sources should lead to an easier decision-making process.

A multitude of studies have indicated that the most common—and dangerous—types of adverse events in hospitalized patients are adverse drug events, hospital-acquired infections, and surgical complications. It will be important to review and prioritize data related to these variables when considering your local facilities. While adverse drug events and surgical complications are self-explanatory, I want to mention a few things about hospital-acquired infections (HAIs), which are infections acquired in the hospital and not present at the time of admission. The Centers for Disease Control and Prevention (CDC) reports nearly 1.7 million hospitalized patients annually with hospital-acquired infections resulting in 98,000 patient deaths.[19] These staggering figures highlight a challenge faced around the world. For a global perspective, consider this: if you have 100 patients in a hospital in a wealthier country, about 7 of them will contract an infection during their stay. In less wealthy countries, the number is higher—about 15 out of 100. Alarmingly, 1 in 10 patients with these infections will not survive.[20] So, you can see just how serious and significant this issue is. Many of the resources below provide comprehensive statistics on infection-related variables and other relevant information for the facilities you might be researching.

1. **Consumer Advocacy Groups**
   A. Hospital Leapfrog Survey (https://ratings.leapfroggroup.org) is one of the two programs offered under the Leapfrog Group, a nonprofit organization that guides and advocates for healthcare consumers by increasing transparency in healthcare. They request over 2,000 hospitals to voluntarily report on measures of interest through an annual survey on safety, quality, and resource use. You can compare different hospitals

with their performances on measures related to preventing and responding to patient harm, billing ethics, critical care staffing, healthcare-associated infections, maternity care, medication safety, and information about various surgical procedures. I like that you can see exactly how many surgical procedures they've performed over the past year. If you need to have a heart valve surgery or orthopedic procedure, it may be worthwhile to compare the different facilities in your area to see which has the most experience with a procedure. It also provides information on how a facility ranks in terms of healthcare-associated infections, which, as mentioned above, is a very important factor in increasing the risk of harm and death to hospitalized patients.

B. Leapfrog Hospital Safety Grade (https://www. hospitalsafetygrade.org/) is the second program under the Leapfrog Group, exclusively covering safety variables, such as accidents, injuries, and errors, and assigns a safety grade from A to F based on the results of the survey and data from the Centers for Medicare & Medicaid Services. It provides an easy-to-search platform that allows you to put in your city and state. It then provides a list of many of the local hospitals and their associated grades.

I also like that they show grades from past years for each medical center so you can see if improvements are being made. After viewing the overall grade, you can look under specific areas of interest, such as prevention of patient harm, critical care, healthcare-associated infections, maternity or pediatric care, or elective surgery measures, to see how well a particular facility compares to other hospitals in the area.

2. Government Agencies

Another resource provided by the Centers for Medicare & Medicaid Services is called Hospital Compare (https://www.medicare.gov/hospitalcompare/search.html), which provides information on quality variables at Medicare-certified hospitals. They provide an overall Star Rating, complications and mortality rates, and information on readmission rates and payments for care with a comparison to the national average. I like this site as it has separate overall and patient ratings for multiple types of facilities, such as hospitals, nursing homes, dialysis centers, and even home health services. I found the patient ratings (versus the overall ratings) more aligned with my own experiences in different facilities across Los Angeles. If a patient survey Star Rating is low, you can click and learn more about the variables that caused the low marks, such as communication from doctors and nurses, explanations of new medications from staff, cleanliness and quietness of a room, and percentage of patients who would recommend the hospital to others.

3. State Health Department

You can check your state's health department website for information specific to your region. Examples of these include the California Department of Public Health (CDPH) at https://www.cdph.ca.gov. On this website, I like the specific details given on hospitals, such as number of beds, ratings, or specific complaints or incidents reported on a wide variety of facility types, such as acute-care hospitals, nursing homes, hospice facilities, etc. Another example is NYS Health Profiles, put together by the New York State Department of Health (https://profiles.health.

ny.gov/hospital/index). It offers similar quality and safety measures information in an easy-to-read, color-coded chart. It also includes reports on the quality of care provided by different types of health settings, such as nursing homes, home care agencies, and hospices.

4. Hospital Websites

Many hospitals are required to publicly report certain quality and safety measures on their websites. Look for sections like "Quality and Safety" or "Patient Information." They may provide data on readmissions, mortality rates, and infection rates.

5. Healthcare Rating Websites

You can check websites like Healthgrades (https://www. healthgrades.com) and U.S. News & World Report (https:// health.usnews.com/best-hospitals) to see how hospitals are rated. These sites provide easy-to-understand rankings and information about hospitals, helping you find the best one for your needs. They look at things like how well patients do after treatment and what services hospitals offer.

6. Hospital Accreditation Organizations

Organizations like The Joint Commission often accredit hospitals based on certain quality and safety standards. You can visit their website (https://www.jointcommission. org) to check whether a hospital is accredited and view related information.

When researching hospital quality and safety data, it's crucial to emphasize the significance of consulting multiple sources and seeking the latest available data. By staying informed and asking questions, you empower yourself as a patient or advocate.

TEACHABLE POINTS

1. **Hospital Selection Matters:** Just like we research products before buying, it's crucial to research hospitals and medical facilities, as they vary in quality and services.

2. **Access Appropriate Care:** Choose the right hospital type based on your healthcare needs. Make sure you have easy access to it in times of need.

3. **Hospital Profit Models:** Consider the benefits of nonprofit or for-profit models as suitable for your personal needs. Nonprofit hospitals prioritize patient outcomes and community well-being, while for-profit hospitals may have greater financial resources for innovation and a competitiveness that can improve healthcare quality and options.

4. **Teaching versus Nonteaching Hospitals:** Consider teaching hospitals for advanced and complex care, highly specialized physicians, and access to cutting-edge research. Consider nonteaching hospitals for a more streamlined and personalized experience, potentially lower costs, and a possible advantage for routine healthcare needs.

5. **Hospital Size Matters:** In most cases, the size of a hospital correlates with the range of services it can provide. Smaller hospitals are well suited for basic medical needs, while larger ones tend to offer more comprehensive and specialized services, making them suitable for complex cases. Note that exceptions exist.

6. **Medical Errors Statistics:** It's important to recognize that medical errors may be underreported due to factors

like fear of repercussions, a blame culture, and a lack of feedback mechanisms. This issue can significantly impact the accuracy of safety statistics.

7. **Quality Metrics Matter:** Research and select a hospital that not only ranks high in terms of expertise, resources, and patient care but also excels in terms of low complications, healthcare-associated infections, readmissions, and other quality metrics.

8. **Utilize Multiple Resources:** When researching hospitals, use a variety of sources, including consumer advocacy groups, government agencies, state health departments, hospital websites, healthcare rating sites, and accreditation organizations like The Joint Commission.

Chapter 2

KNOW YOUR OUTPATIENT PROVIDERS

In Chapter 1 we discussed how the quality and safety of hospitals can play an important role in the midst of a health emergency. In setting out to find your ideal healthcare team, it's critical to prioritize the search for a primary care provider who aligns with your needs and values. This provider is your primary point of contact for health concerns, knows your medical history intimately, and acts as a gatekeeper for specialist referrals. During critical situations, your primary care provider guides decisions that will hopefully clarify the need for emergency room visits or hospital admissions.

If you require a visit to the hospital, your primary care doctor may play a pivotal role by passing on important details about your medical history, how you reacted to medications, any past abnormal test results or scans, and the outcomes of any medical procedures or referrals, even if they happened a while ago or at different hospitals. This type of communication is a tremendous help for the hospital doctors, especially considering their limited time and the number of new patients they meet. It helps them understand your situation better, focus on what's important, and efficiently provide treatments that fit your needs and preferences.

You might be questioning the need to have a general primary care provider when your health primarily revolves around a specialist, such as a cardiologist or nephrologist. Why would someone with a history of heart attacks or heart failure need to consult a primary care provider instead of exclusively relying on a specialist?

The reason: Primary care providers are exceptionally well equipped to address, prevent, diagnose, treat, and prioritize a broad spectrum of medical conditions. While the expertise of a cardiologist, for instance, is invaluable in managing heart-related issues, it's essential to recognize that most specialists typically concentrate on their field of expertise and may not be as attuned to addressing conditions beyond their specialties.

I'll always remember our family hematologist's stressed tone of voice whenever we brought up concerns related to an organ outside his field of expertise. If we had a kidney-related question, he'd promptly remind us, "I'm not a kidney doctor," and urge us to seek guidance from the appropriate specialist. So, while your specialist can provide excellent and focused care for a particular condition or organ system, they're less likely to focus on the high-level view of all your health concerns. In contrast, your primary care provider should provide more comprehensive care, including preventive screenings, immunizations, and guidance on lifestyle interventions like nutrition, exercise, and stress management. They should also integrate information from all your specialists, bridge gaps in your healthcare, promote overall well-being, prevent serious health issues, and improve your quality of life and long-term health.

PRIMARY CARE PROVIDERS

Amid unprecedented shortages of primary care providers—due to a lower percentage of medical residents and trainees entering primary care residencies, early retirement, significant physician burnout, etc.—many patients will be required to see nonphysician providers for their primary care needs. These nonphysician providers— often called advanced practice providers, physician extenders, or midlevel providers—typically include physician assistants (PAs) and nurse practitioners (NPs). They assess, diagnose, and treat patients but don't have the extensive education required of physicians.

Many medical centers and hospitals had hoped that by replacing physicians with nonphysicians, such as physician assistants or nurse practitioners, they could provide the same service at a lower cost. However, recent analysis and research in this area has created some food for thought. A leading private multispecialty clinic in south Mississippi, Hattiesburg Clinic, has reviewed quality and cost data over a 10-year period, looking at 300 physicians, 150 nonphysician providers, and 200,000 patient surveys, and found some interesting patterns.[1]

Looking at variables such as quality, cost, patient experience, and utilization (such as frequency of referral to emergency rooms and specialists), physician-led care teams had improved measures across the board. Interestingly, this report showed that the patients of nonphysician providers were more likely to visit the emergency room than those with physician primary care providers. This in no way implies that nonphysician providers aren't providing a critical role and need. Instead, it suggests that the best outcomes are associated with a team of providers who work together effectively. In fact, the same study showed that comanaging patients in a primary care setting, defined as having alternating visits with the physician and a nurse or physician's assistant, showed the best outcomes in quality and cost overall.

A few words on why it's crucial to differentiate between various titles, roles, training, and kinds of experience in the healthcare system.

Providers frequently fail or don't take the time to provide patients with a detailed explanation of their roles or titles. Some may look like doctors, wear white coats, or carry stethoscopes, leading patients to think they're speaking with a physician when, in fact, qualifications and roles may vary significantly. I've seen situations in which providers use the title *Doctor* or *Dr.* before their name when introducing themselves, on their websites, or on social media, creating a misleading impression that they're qualified medical providers capable of offering medical treatment and advice. This is why it's so important to not only know whom you're talking to but also understand the strengths and limitations of their education, training, and experience. In today's healthcare landscape, the term *doctor* is used more loosely than ever, leading to ambiguity and confusion.

Taking this one step further, I've even seen the infrequent chiropractor, acupuncturist, health coach, nutritionist, or herbalist refer to themselves as a doctor, misrepresenting their roles. Even without these incidents of misrepresentation, patients sometimes designate alternative care providers as their primary providers. This can potentially lead to concerning consequences.

Having attended acupuncture school and chiropractor-aimed medical conferences myself, I realized that, in terms of education and knowledge, alternative medicine training is vastly different from traditional medical training. Unfortunately, I've had the misfortune of witnessing questionable care from some of these providers. This isn't at all due to the provider's ill intentions but rather a lack of extensive training and awareness of the gaps in their education compared to medical doctors.

Bottom line: Doctors are best trained to identify life-threatening conditions due to their rigorous medical education, training, and clinical experience. I believe advanced practice providers, such as PAs and NPs, although they may have fewer years of clinical training hours, can accumulate substantial clinical experience in the years post-training and become well trained to recognize medical emergencies. While alternative medicine providers, like acupuncturists, homeopaths, or herbalists, may be better trained to optimize wellness and prevention, they're not a substitute for the acute-care expertise of primary care providers. For these reasons, I advise that you not forgo a primary care provider.

In the context of this book, which focuses on adult patients and their potential hospital needs, I list below the most common primary care provider types, years of training and scope of practice.[2]

1. Family Practitioner (Family Medicine Physician)

— Degree: Doctor of Medicine (MD) or Doctor of Osteopathic Medicine (DO)
— Undergraduate Education: Typically 4 years
— Medical School: 4 years
— Residency Training: 3 years in family medicine
— Total Years of Training: Approximately 11
— Clinical Training Hours: Varies, but often includes rotations in family medicine, pediatrics, obstetrics, and other areas (approximately 12,000 to 16,000)
— Scope: Provides comprehensive care for patients of all ages, from infants to seniors, emphasizing preventive care, wellness, and treatment of acute and chronic illnesses

Note: MDs and DOs are both medical doctors with similar training and scope of practice. DOs receive additional training in osteopathic manipulative medicine, which involves hands-on techniques for diagnosis and treatment.

2. Internist (Internal Medicine Physician)

— Degree: Doctor of Medicine (MD) or Doctor of Osteopathic Medicine (DO)
— Undergraduate Education: Typically 4 years
— Medical School: 4 years
— Residency Training: 3 years in internal medicine
— Total Years of Training: Approximately 11
— Clinical Training Hours: Varies, but with a focus on adult patients (approximately 12,000 to 16,000)
— Scope: Specializes in the prevention, diagnosis, and treatment of adult diseases, often managing complex medical conditions

3. Geriatrician

— Degree: Doctor of Medicine (MD) or Doctor of Osteopathic Medicine (DO)
— Undergraduate Education: Typically 4 years
— Medical School: 4 years
— Residency Training: 3 years in internal medicine plus 1 to 2 years in geriatric medicine
— Total Years of Training: Approximately 12 to 13
— Clinical Training Hours: Focused on elderly patients, with a focus on age-related health issues (approximately 12,000 to 16,000+)
— Scope: Specializes in the healthcare of older adults (typically 65 and older), addressing age-related medical and social issues, managing multiple chronic conditions, and improving the overall well-being of seniors

4. Nurse Practitioner (NP)

— Degree: Master of Science in Nursing (MSN) or Doctor of Nursing Practice (DNP)
— Nursing Education: Typically 4 years for Bachelor of Science in Nursing (BSN)
— Advanced Nursing Education: 2 to 4 years for MSN or DNP (online-only programs accepted)
— Clinical Training Hours: Approximately 500 to 1,000 (varies by program and state)
— Scope: Specializes in various patient populations, such as family, adult-gerontology, pediatrics, or women's health; provides primary care services, including health assessments, diagnosis, treatment, and patient education

5. Physician Assistant (PA)

— Degree: Master's degree (typically Master of Physician Assistant Studies)
— Undergraduate Education: Typically 4 years
— Physician Assistant Program: 2 to 3 years
— Clinical Training Hours: Approximately 2,000 during the program
— Scope: Trained as a generalist but can work in various specialties; provides diagnostic, therapeutic, and preventive healthcare services, often working alongside physicians

6. Naturopathic Doctor (ND)

— Degree: Doctor of Naturopathy (ND)
— Education: Requires completion of a 4-year naturopathic medical program accredited by the Council on Naturopathic Medical Education (CNME)
— Clinical Training: Approximately 1,200 to 1,500 hours emphasizing nutrition, botanical medicine, lifestyle counseling, and holistic approaches, with less emphasis on hospital and pharmaceutical medicine
— Scope: Focuses on holistic and natural healthcare approaches, emphasizing prevention and addressing root causes
— Acceptance as PCP: Accepted as primary care providers in some states, allowing them to diagnose, treat, and manage various health conditions; check state-specific regulations for details. However, their prescribing rights vary significantly by state. While some states allow NDs broad prescribing privileges, including most pharmaceuticals, others limit them to a specific list of medications or prohibit the prescription of conventional pharmaceuticals altogether.

CHOOSING A PRIMARY CARE PROVIDER (PCP)

Selecting the right primary care provider is a highly personal choice, and there's no one-size-fits-all answer. Your PCP plays a crucial role in your healthcare journey, serving as your first point of contact for medical concerns. To make an informed decision, it's essential to consider various factors. Here are some useful tips to help guide your selection process:

1. **Evaluate Their Credentials:** Review their qualifications, certifications, and medical training. You can also consider checking the rankings of the colleges and medical schools they attended to assess their educational background. Confirm that they hold the necessary licenses and are board-certified in their specialty.

2. **Assess Clinical Experience:** Consider their years in clinical practice. More experience can deepen their understanding of various medical conditions, while newer providers may bring the latest medical knowledge. It's important to balance experience with staying updated.

3. **Review Work History:** Look into their work history, including any affiliations with hospitals or healthcare institutions. This can give you insights into their professional network.

4. **Specialized Expertise:** Use websites, social media, and the Internet to assess their interests and areas of medical expertise. This can be particularly helpful if you have specific healthcare needs, allowing you to choose a PCP whose expertise aligns with your requirements.

5. **Check for Disciplinary Actions:** Research their background to confirm there are no disciplinary actions associated with their medical licenses. Sources to consider include state medical and nursing boards.

6. **Accessibility and Availability:** Inquire about availability for scheduling appointments, handling urgent issues, and communicating with the provider or support staff, as these factors can impact your overall experience.

7. **Practice Size:** Assess whether the PCP is affiliated with a larger group or operates as a solo practitioner. Your choice should align with your healthcare needs and preferences. Larger groups may provide enhanced resources and better coverage during emergencies, especially if you have complex medical needs. Conversely, smaller practices may provide a more personalized touch with fewer staff and more direct access to the provider.

8. **Communication Style:** Evaluate their communication skills and approachability. A good PCP should listen to your concerns and explain medical matters clearly.

9. **Testimonials and Recommendations:** Read patient reviews and testimonials to gauge the PCP's reputation and patient satisfaction. Seek advice and recommendations from friends, family, and colleagues who might have insights into different providers.

10. **Location:** Choose a PCP with a convenient location to ensure ease of access for regular checkups and appointments.

11. **Insurance Coverage:** Verify that your chosen provider accepts your health insurance to minimize out-of-pocket expenses.

12. **Emergency Protocols:** Ask about their policies for after-hours or weekend care. Inquire about their emergency procedures and hospital affiliations and privileges for seamless care coordination during a hospitalization.

13. **Cultural and Religious Compatibility:** If finding a PCP aligned with your cultural and religious beliefs, especially if they impact your healthcare decisions, is important to you, discuss these preferences during initial consultations to ensure compatibility.

14. **Language Proficiency:** Seek a PCP who speaks your language fluently or provides access to interpretation services if English isn't your first language. Effective communication is crucial for understanding your medical conditions, treatment options, and preventive care.

15. **Interview Providers:** Arrange consultations or meet-and-greet appointments with several PCPs to ask questions about their medical approach and experience with your specific health concerns.

16. **Visit the Office:** If possible, visit the PCP's office to evaluate the environment and staff, as a welcoming and organized office can contribute to a positive experience.

17. **Openness to Second Opinions:** When evaluating potential PCPs, inquire about their stance on second opinions. A provider who encourages and supports you in seeking additional expertise, when necessary, demonstrates a commitment to ensuring you receive the

most appropriate and effective treatments, regardless of the source.

18. **Patient Engagement and Shared Decision-Making:** Inquire about the PCP's approach to involving patients in their healthcare decisions. A provider who values shared decision-making and encourages your active participation can enhance the quality of your healthcare experience.

19. **Preventive Care and Wellness Programs:** Ask about the PCP's approach to preventive care and wellness. Providers who emphasize preventive measures and offer wellness programs can play a crucial role in helping you maintain good health.

20. **Chronic Disease Management:** If you have a chronic medical condition, discuss the PCP's experience and approach to managing such conditions. Effective management of chronic illnesses requires a proactive and comprehensive approach.

21. **Electronic Health Records (EHRs) and Telemedicine:** Inquire about their use of electronic health records and whether they offer telemedicine services. EHRs can improve coordination of care, and telemedicine can provide convenient access to healthcare, especially for follow-up appointments or minor consultations.

22. **Concierge Practices:** Some PCPs offer concierge or direct primary care services, where patients pay an annual fee for enhanced access, personalized care, and maybe a more aesthetically pleasing office environment. These practices often have smaller patient panels, which can mean more attentive service, longer appointment times, and help with referrals. However, keep in mind that

more money doesn't necessarily guarantee better care. Evaluate whether a concierge practice aligns with your preferences and budget, as it can offer a unique approach to primary care.

23. **Trust Your Instincts:** Ultimately, trust your instincts in choosing a PCP. If you don't feel a connection or have doubts about a particular one, it's perfectly acceptable to continue your search until you find the right fit.

PCP VERSUS HOSPITAL DOCTOR

While the traditional practice of your PCP attending to you in the hospital is becoming less common in many places, it's important to understand your options. It's worth asking your PCP whether they offer hospital care services or have arrangements to visit and care for you during a hospitalization. Some doctors in the US still provide this personalized hospital care, and according to 2013 Medicare data, PCPs cared for their own patients in approximately 14% of hospital admissions.[3] Nowadays, however, hospitalists (specialized doctors dedicated to hospital care) typically oversee your treatment in the hospital. Studies show that hospitalists are highly skilled at efficiently navigating hospital systems and providing care for serious illnesses. What they miss out on by not knowing all your medical history in detail and not having a long-term personal relationship is replaced by a much more skilled and efficient navigation of the hospital system. Patients being cared for by hospitalists often have shorter lengths of stay than those cared for by their personal outpatient doctors, who are less accustomed to taking care of serious illnesses on a day-to-day basis.[4]

PROVIDER REVIEWS

A word about various resources that provide reviews on different providers: I mentioned that it's worthwhile to investigate and compare different providers' medical school training and job experience. You can often find this information on the doctor's website or, if they're part of a larger organization, on the medical center's website. There's no magic formula that will ensure you find the perfect provider just based on the medical school or training program they attended, but it's a good start. I've seen questionable practices from doctors who came from the best US training programs and exceptional care from graduates of foreign schools or training programs I've never heard of. In fact, in some cases, the medical students and doctors who trained outside the US have gone through a more rigorous process in their respective countries.

There's an ever-growing list of online sources where you can check for reviews on providers. Some of these are Healthgrades, Vitals, Yelp, Google Business Profile, RateMDs, and Zocdoc. While these can be helpful, there are often major reliability issues with these sources due to their subjective and biased nature. I've often noticed that unsatisfied patients can sometimes be the most active in writing reviews. In some instances, the negative experiences that prompt these bad reviews seem to stem from nonmedical factors, such as less-than-ideal interactions with office staff, poor reimbursement from an insurance carrier, or other factors that have nothing to do with the physician directly. To get a more balanced perspective, use reviews cautiously and consider multiple sources. These days, more and more providers are becoming active on social media, using sites like Facebook or Instagram to express their views and opinions. These sources, along with online videos, webinars, or even podcasts, may give greater insight into a provider's experience and interests.

Your research is simply a starting point for collecting data from different sources.

After looking at a few online reviews, asking for recommendations from providers you trust, and getting feedback from friends and family who have firsthand experience with a particular doctor, you should have an easier time finding a solution that works for you.

TEACHABLE POINTS

1. **Your PCP's Role:** Recognize that your PCP is like the quarterback of your healthcare team, coordinating your overall care, understanding your medical history, and guiding you to specialists when needed. They can also be your advocate in the hospital by sharing with the hospital team important information about your health, past treatments, and medication reactions.

2. **PCP versus Specialist:** Realize that while specialists are experts in their fields, they may not focus on your overall health. A PCP will provide comprehensive care, including preventive checkups, vaccinations, and advice on staying healthy.

3. **Teams Provide Better Care:** Understand the importance of different healthcare providers working together as a team to give you the best care.

4. **Understanding Provider Titles:** Be aware of the various titles and roles in healthcare so you can make informed decisions and avoid misunderstandings.

5. **Spot Misrepresentation:** Learn how to recognize when providers may misrepresent themselves as something they're not and why it matters for your safety.

6. **Training Differences Matter:** Understand that physicians, advanced-level practitioners (like NPs and PAs), and alternative medicine providers all differ in the length, depth, and focus of their education, training, and clinical experience. These factors impact your care and need to align with your health goals.

7. **Choosing a PCP:** Know the important considerations for finding a PCP who aligns with your values to ensure the best experience.

Chapter 3

GET YOUR RECORDS IN ORDER

By now, you've researched local hospitals and assembled your team of doctors, which is no small feat. Yet, if I had to emphasize one topic as one of the most crucial in this book, it would be the subject of this chapter.

We'll dive deep into understanding some very important documents that indicate your preferences regarding lifesaving treatment and designate your decision-makers. We'll also explore best practices for recordkeeping, starting with advance directives.

ADVANCE DIRECTIVES

Maybe you're reading this book to help an older family member with health concerns. Maybe you're planning for yourself. Whichever applies, it's a good idea for *all* adults to have an advance directive because we never know when our health can take an unexpected turn. So, if you're helping someone fill out theirs, do the same for yourself if you don't already have one.

Despite the importance of this document, it's estimated that nearly two-thirds of people don't have one.[1] Advance directives ensure your wishes are honored in unexpected health situations, and they're the best way to express how you want to live and be treated, especially if you can't speak for yourself. The specific requirements and content of these documents may vary from state to state and may include living wills, healthcare proxies, Do Not Resuscitate (DNR) forms, or Portable Medical Orders (POLST). Most commonly, advance directives contain two parts:

- Living will: Specifies your desired treatments if you are not able to communicate them during a medical emergency.
- Healthcare proxy: Designates a person who can make medical decisions for you if you're unable to do so.

Remember, completing these forms is crucial, but ensuring they are easily accessible is just as important. Keep copies in a secure yet accessible place, and make sure that your healthcare proxy, family members, and primary care physician know where to find them. This will help avoid any delays in honoring your wishes should an emergency arise.

In many states, completing the forms is quite simple and may not even require a lawyer. You can use this resource, https://www.caringinfo.org/planning/advance-directives/by-state/, as a good starting point and download the appropriate forms. Here are the steps to follow:

- Review the forms and take notes on any questions.
- Have open discussions with your healthcare providers, especially your PCP, to assess your health risks and align treatments with your goals.

- After discussion with your healthcare team and family, complete the forms. Some documents may require the signatures of witnesses to be legally valid.
- Print or store them digitally.

Advance directives never expire, but you can change yours as often as you like. Consider reviewing and possibly making new advance directives when facing a significant new health diagnosis, getting a divorce, or approximately every five to ten years to ensure they align with your current preferences. Any change in documentation, of course, needs to be shared with your PCP and loved ones. Please note that advance directives may not be universally valid across states, so if you spend time in multiple states, consider completing directives for each separately.

While reviewing your documents every few years, it's also smart to check that they still comply with current state laws. A quick check-in with a legal professional or a healthcare advocate can give you peace of mind that your paperwork is legally sound and will be honored when needed.

While much of this documentation has traditionally been on paper, these days, a lot of digital websites make the process even easier. Some have easy-to-use software for recording digital or video advance directives. Some resources include the following:

- MyDirectives.com: MyDirectives offers an easy way to draft a comprehensive advance care plan without cost. You can provide details about your wishes and are even able to include video messages. The site states that your plan can be shared readily and is accessible to connected hospitals upon admission. Adjustments and updates to your plan are easy to make. On average, appointing a healthcare agent or proxy takes about two minutes, and creating a complete digital advance care plan takes around 20 minutes.

- PrepareforYourCare.org: The PREPARE programs, developed at the University of California, San Francisco (UCSF), offer free and easy-to-follow videos and stories, which can guide you through making healthcare choices that are right for you. The programs also enjoy support from the Leukemia and Lymphoma Society.
- Vitaldecisions.mylivingvoice.com: My Living Voice, offered by Vital Decisions and a part of Evolent Health, present a secure online method for creating an Advanced Healthcare Directive. This user-friendly service walks you through the process, and in about ten minutes, you can have a legally recognized directive once it's signed and verified. These directives can then be shared with hospitals to ensure your medical wishes are known.

Important Note: Please keep in mind that your advance directives won't be effective during a medical emergency, except for identifying your healthcare agent. In an emergency, the ambulance and emergency department staff are obligated to perform cardiopulmonary resuscitation (CPR), which may involve chest compressions, oxygen, and shocks to your heart, unless you have a separate document called the Do Not Resuscitate (DNR) or Portable Medical Orders (POLST) (see more details below). These forms inform paramedics and emergency department providers regarding a person's wishes with respect to CPR or certain lifesaving measures if their heart stops. Both forms must be signed by the person or their chosen healthcare agent *and* their doctors to confirm that the decision was well informed. Both should be kept close to the person so medical teams can find it quickly.

One final point regarding advance directives: While they're legal documents that make your wishes clear to those caring for you, doctors aren't legally bound to follow them if they're medically inappropriate. This is another reason regular conversations with your doctors are important to make sure your wishes are appropriate considering your specific health issues.

The High Stakes of Not Having Advance Directives:
A Cautionary Tale[2]

I recently read a compelling story in the Washington Post *about Douglas Hulse, a story that shows what can happen when you don't have advance directives in place. Douglas, a former pilot, suffered a stroke and was left unable to communicate his wishes or make financial decisions. Since no one could reach his family and he had no advance directive or healthcare proxy named, the hospital was placed in a difficult position. To manage his care and affairs, they initiated a legal process to have someone make decisions for him—this is known as guardianship or conservatorship.*

In such situations, a judge appoints a guardian or conservator who is tasked with making all kinds of critical choices for the patient—choices about healthcare, living arrangements, and even financial matters. This person could be granted the authority to access the patient's confidential information and bank accounts, consent to or refuse medical treatment, manage or sell assets like a home—which in Douglas's case, was sold for less than its value.

It's a sobering reminder that not having advance directives can lead to someone else making life-altering decisions on your behalf. It highlights why it's critical to take charge of your future by documenting your healthcare preferences and choosing someone you trust to act as your healthcare proxy.

LIVING WILL

A living will is a legal document that outlines your preferences for medical treatments to keep you alive and other end-of-life care decisions, like nutrition, pain management, and organ donation. When considering your living will, keep in mind that your responses to these questions, as well as how well you may recover from various lifesaving treatments, depend significantly on factors like your age, existing health conditions, and baseline level of functioning. For example, if you're in your forties and are generally in good health but experience a sudden heart attack, your decisions may differ from those of an individual in their eighties who has preexisting heart disease and is undergoing dialysis. These factors highlight the importance of consulting with a healthcare professional who knows your medical history well. Only they can provide a well-informed discussion about the real risks and benefits in complex medical situations. Your PCP and specialists are typically the best points of contact for these important conversations. Here are some questions to think about:

1. **Understanding Life Support:** Have you talked to your doctor about the machines and treatments they might

use if you're very sick and need help breathing or your heart stops?

2. **Mechanical Ventilation (or Breathing Machine**): Would you want to be placed on a machine to help with breathing if you were unable to breathe on your own? If so, under what circumstances and for how long? Do you understand the risks of prolonged ventilation?

3. **Tube Feeding:** How would you feel about having a stomach tube or intravenous catheter to provide nutrients and fluids if you were unable to swallow on your own? Under what conditions would you accept this, and for how long?

4. **Dialysis:** If your kidneys no longer function, do you want to receive dialysis? If so, when and for how long?

5. **Prolonging Life:** Do you want doctors to use all available methods to keep you alive, no matter what? Or are there conditions under which you'd prefer they didn't continue treatment?

6. **Quality of Life:** Consider what circumstances might make you feel life is no longer worth living. What things matter most to you? Do you want to keep doing certain activities, like walking, talking, or eating on your own?

7. **Spiritual and Religious Preferences:** Are there any special spiritual or religious practices you'd want if you were very sick?

8. **Where to Receive Care or Pass Away:** If you could choose, where would you like to get medical care? At

home, in a hospital, or somewhere else? Where would you like to spend your final moments?

9. **Final Arrangements:** Have you decided whether you want to be buried or cremated?

10. **Organ Donation Decision:** Would you like to give your organs to help others after you're gone?

HEALTHCARE PROXY

This refers to documents you use to appoint a person to make medical decisions for you if you're unable to do so. For example, if you were involved in a serious car accident with head trauma, needed urgent surgery, or were put on life support, it would be critical that you have on record an individual to make medical decisions for you. This may or may not be part of the advance directive paperwork in your state. Also, depending on the state you live in, the person you choose can be called various terms, such as healthcare agent, healthcare proxy, healthcare representative, or surrogate.

Choosing this person is very important. Not only must they meet your state's requirements for a healthcare agent, but they need to be a trusted advocate for you who can make medical decisions on your behalf that align with your expressed wishes and values. Once again, to keep the burden and confusion of all these challenging decision-making choices from falling on your loved ones, it helps to discuss your wishes in advance with your health surrogates and document them for future reference.

I've witnessed numerous occasions when family members, children, and siblings had different opinions about what to do for a loved one in the hospital. A serious hospitalization is a huge stressor on any family or individual, and when family members disagree, things can become very uncomfortable. I've often seen this when children don't agree with the goals of care for hospitalized elderly parents. Designating a health surrogate or proxy relieves the frustration and confusion that can arise during challenging medical situations.

I have a physician friend who got around this tough issue with an interesting solution: instead of naming family members as decision-makers, he listed three physician friends as his healthcare representatives. The majority decision between those doctors would be the implemented decision. While we may not all have three physician friends, we can entrust healthcare decisions to people who aren't family members if they're more appropriate.

It's important to realize that a healthcare agent or proxy can't take away your rights or override your decisions. If you're alert and mentally competent, you always have the legal right to override your proxy's decision or revoke the directive.

However, if you don't name an agent or proxy, and family members disagree, the situation could require a court-appointed guardian. Choosing a healthcare proxy is one of the most important decisions you'll make. It should be someone who knows you very well, with whom you have discussed your values, goals, and preferences, and who can handle the decision-making responsibility as your spokesperson and advocate. It's recommended that a copy of the document remain with your medical provider.

PREHOSPITAL DO NOT RESUSCITATE ORDERS AND POLST

In the event of an emergency, 911 is typically called. Paramedics attempt to resuscitate the patient, then transport them to the nearest hospital, where lifesaving measures are provided to stabilize them. The patient may then be transferred to the ICU for aggressive lifesaving interventions without adequate time to check for an advance directive. While time is often of the essence and may not allow for a thorough search, paramedics may look for identifiable DNR or POLST forms upon arrival or during transport. If a Prehospital Do Not Resuscitate (DNR) Order or Portable Medical Order (POLST) is readily available and visible, the family can provide first responders with a copy, or it may be found in a common location such as on the refrigerator or with the patient's identification. These two forms are very important medical orders that instruct emergency medical technicians (EMTs), paramedics, and other emergency personnel on the patient's wishes if their heart or breathing stops.

PREHOSPITAL DO NOT RESUSCITATE (DNR) ORDER

Emergency personnel are trained to save lives and will do so unless directed otherwise by a valid DNR order. If you have a serious illness or are at a point where you do not wish to have lifesaving treatments, a DNR order informs emergency personnel not to perform CPR, including chest compressions, assisted ventilations, intubation, defibrillation, or heart medication administration. It also indicates that you can still receive other forms of necessary medical care. If you decide to revoke your DNR, it's essential to inform your healthcare providers directly. It does require a doctor's signature to be valid. To find out about the specifics of these forms and where to obtain them, consult your healthcare providers, since the details can vary from state to state.

PORTABLE MEDICAL ORDERS (POLST)

The Portable Medical Orders, also referred to as Physician Orders for Life-Sustaining Treatment (POLST), form is more detailed than the DNR orders and typically used for severely ill or frail patients who may have an unexpected health emergency outside the hospital. It has four main sections:

1. Cardiopulmonary Resuscitation (CPR): This section asks what you want or don't want in case of an emergency. You can select either (a) Attempt Resuscitation/CPR, which means to deliver all lifesaving interventions, like chest compressions, breathing tube, and medications, or (b) Do Not Attempt Resuscitation.

2. Medical Orders for Life-Sustaining Treatment: This section asks you to indicate details about the level of medical intervention you desire, such as (a) full treatment, or prolonging life by all means possible, such as chest compressions, shock, breathing machine, etc., (b) limited treatment, which may include antibiotics, fluids, and other medical treatments as appropriate; however, it requests the withholding of intubation or connection to a breathing machine, or (c) comfort-focused care, which has the primary goals of maximizing comfort, decreasing pain, and alleviating suffering using medication administered through any necessary route. This care can be provided at home or wherever paramedics arrive. If necessary, it can also involve transfer to a hospital for continued comfort-focused care.

3. Artificially Administered Nutrition: This part addresses whether you want artificial nutrition (such as feeding tubes) and hydration (intravenous fluids) or if you prefer to avoid them.

4. Other Wishes and Signature: Here you can include any additional instructions or preferences, such as organ donation wishes. The form is typically signed by a healthcare provider and sometimes by the patient or their legal representative to make it legally binding.

UNDERSTANDING CODE STATUS DOCUMENTATION

While the prehospital DNR and POLST forms are useful documentation for those who may be more ill or have unexpected emergencies at home or outside of the hospital or healthcare setting, understanding the same concepts is also relevant to anyone who requires hospitalization. In this situation, it's referred to as designating code status, or in-hospital DNR orders. These orders are used within a hospital or healthcare facility when a patient is already admitted. They guide healthcare providers on whether or not to perform cardiopulmonary resuscitation (CPR) if the patient's heart stops or they stop breathing while in the hospital. Depending on your wishes, your medical chart will be marked with one of these options:

Full Code: Indicates all resuscitation efforts will be provided to keep you alive (i.e., chest compressions, breathing machine, and shock if needed). Full code status is best for individuals who are generally healthy or don't have advanced medical conditions.

Limited Code: This means that only specific resuscitation procedures will be used during a medical emergency. You and your providers should weigh the risks and benefits of different types of medical treatments that would benefit you. For example, someone with advanced lung disease may opt to avoid an intubation or a breathing machine.

DNR (Do Not Resuscitate): DNR doesn't mean "do not treat." A DNR code status indicates that you would be allowed to die naturally if your heart stops beating and/or you stop breathing. Many DNR code status patients still choose to have surgery, chemotherapy, dialysis, artificial nutrition and hydration, and other procedures. DNR status is recommended for people who have multiple chronic illnesses and want to be allowed a natural death.

Comfort Care: This means that only medical treatments that promote comfort will be provided. If you choose comfort care, resuscitation won't be attempted. This status is typically recommended when death is approaching.

In my experience, it often seems that many patients hear about code status for the first time during a hospitalization, which isn't ideal. I believe code status conversations should ideally be introduced gradually during outpatient visits with PCPs. These providers share a stronger and more established relationship with the patient and can engage in these discussions calmly when the patient isn't in a crisis.

It's crucial to understand that choices about code status should be periodically reviewed outside the hospital setting, especially as your medical condition and prognosis change. Even if you've made certain decisions before a hospitalization, you may need to reassess and change them during a single hospitalization, often over a relatively short period. For instance, I was aware of my dad's poor prognosis, but during the first twenty-four to forty-eight hours of his hospitalization, I decided to opt for a limited code status because his condition had changed so suddenly. In a matter of a few hours, he'd gone from participating with a physical therapist and advancing to using stairs to being minimally responsive. Given his reluctance to discuss his end-of-life wishes and his altered mental status during hospitalization, I had to make some difficult decisions. Initially, I believed that a limited code status with chest compressions and shock was a reasonable approach to see if his condition could be quickly reversed. My impression was that connecting him to a breathing machine (intubation) would likely lead to prolonged complications and recovery in the ICU, a situation that wouldn't result in optimal recovery and survival. Imagine my shock when, a couple of days into his hospital stay and after becoming much more alert, he expressed to his doctors his desire to be a full code.

Each year, approximately 290,000 or more US hospitalized patients are treated for cardiac arrests, and studies indicate only 25% of patients survive to discharge.[3] Cardiac arrests occur most frequently in the ICU, with a significant percentage suffering from a risk of rib fractures and neurologic disability from CPR. In a study of patients aged 65 and older who experienced in-hospital events, those with cardiac arrests occurring beyond the first three days had lower survival rates, worse neurological outcomes among survivors, and longer hospital stays.[4]

The bottom line is that leaving the decision regarding code status and resuscitation to family during a medical crisis, when the patient is unstable or unable to answer for themselves, often leads to decisions made out of fear and lack of knowledge.

While some families choose to prolong their loved one's life regardless of these hardships, these options are often not what a patient would ever choose if they had the ability to pick for themselves, especially in the case of terminal or severe irreversible conditions. A discussion with your team of doctors could further outline the likelihood of meaningful recovery in a situation where life support would be required.

COPIES OF IMPORTANT MEDICAL RECORDS

In addition to the forms and documents discussed earlier, an important bit of advice is to make sure you have easily accessible copies of your most crucial health history, whether in paper or digital form. This will be invaluable in case of a hospital or urgent care visit or when you meet a new doctor. While there's no guarantee that the doctor will have time to review an extensive medical history, it's still wise to have it on hand.

I've had some patients provide me with over 400 pages of medical records and others who couldn't provide the most basic records. Some brought in huge binders filled with labs, X-rays, CT scans, MRI results, and records since their birth. Others have shared documents and sent them via patient portals or email. I recommend having the comprehensive file at home for your own records in case a doctor expresses interest about specific data. The more efficient approach is condensing the important events and contents to no more than two pages. Having a list of diagnoses, surgeries, and relevant or abnormal imaging is a great start and will likely fit on one page. Make sure to include the most updated and accurate medication list, which includes dosage and frequency of use. Allergies and the exact nature of the reaction are other vital and important elements that should be clearly indicated. Far too often, patients report some vague history of allergy from childhood or years past, but they have no recollection of the exact reaction. A mild rash, tongue swelling, and anaphylaxis are very different types of reactions, and it's important to know the specifics.

Add to this list names of primary care doctors, specialists, alternative and complementary medicine providers, and whoever else plays a major role in your care. Speaking of holistic providers, many of them may provide supplements, herbs, and topical and compounded medications that you may not consider relevant when asked for a medication list. However, they're just as important as any other prescription medicine because there may be drug-drug interactions or safety concerns. There have certainly been a handful of cases during my last two decades of practicing hospital medicine where the patient never mentioned herbs or supplements, and that knowledge would have been tremendously helpful in their management and treatment.

TEACHABLE POINTS

1. **Importance of Advance Directives:** Having advance directives, such as a living will and healthcare proxy, is essential to ensure that your healthcare wishes are honored in unexpected situations when you can't communicate them.

2. **Advance Directive Components:** Advance directives commonly include living wills, which describe your desired

treatments during a medical emergency, and healthcare proxies, who are designated people who make medical decisions for you when you can't.

3. **Review Documents:** Advance directives should be reviewed and updated periodically, especially with significant changes in health or personal circumstances, to ensure they align with your current preferences. Communicate changes to your healthcare team and loved ones.

4. **Prehospital DNR and POLST:** These forms guide first responders on your wishes in case of an emergency. They must be signed by both you and your doctors and kept close for quick access.

5. **Code Status:** Familiarize yourself with code status options, like full code, limited code, DNR, and comfort care. Discuss and review these periodically with your PCP and family to ensure your wishes are documented.

6. **Copies of Important Records:** Maintain easily accessible copies of your critical health history, medications, allergies, and healthcare providers' names. Summarize the essential information on one or two pages for convenience.

In the last few chapters, the focus has been on laying the groundwork and foundations you should be thinking about years or decades before an acute medical situation arises. Up next, we'll delve into strategies and considerations that may help you avoid an emergency room visit, as well as practical advice for times when evaluation there becomes necessary.

CHAPTER **4**

WHEN THE HOSPITAL CAN BE AVOIDED AND WHEN IT CAN'T

Not long ago, I received a call from a panicked family member concerning Miriam, a relative with advanced dementia and limited mobility, who was primarily confined to her home. They were asking for my help after a new doctor, temporarily covering for Miriam's primary care physician, urged them to take her to the emergency room. Miriam's Alzheimer's and Parkinson's had significantly progressed over the years, making it increasingly difficult to move her around. Transporting her to medical appointments required so much effort that it took multiple people just to lift her into and out of the car. Also, her deteriorating cognitive and mental health led to frequent episodes of confusion, weakness, anxiety, and drowsiness.

Luckily, we'd established a great medical support system for her years before. Miriam got routine care from a team of doctors and specialists at a teaching facility that took excellent care of her. She had an excellent PCP who knew the details of all medical issues and hospitalizations quite well. She also had a neurologist with expertise in movement disorders who was incredibly knowledgeable about the course of her disease and treatments. Along with a team of other specialists, which included a half dozen other providers, she was taken care of quite comprehensively.

Given her frequent episodes of confusion, the doctor had the home health nurses frequently checking labs or urine tests to monitor her health. On this particular day, the covering doctor, who was unfamiliar with Miriam's case, had become concerned by one of the test results. This concern had prompted the doctor's call urging us to take Miriam to the emergency room for further evaluation. However, after the covering doctor had a brief conversation with me to clarify essential details, the plan took a different course.

When the doctor learned that Miriam had a long history of urinary tract infections that often resolved quickly with antibiotic treatment, they were able to focus on the relevant medical history. In this situation, we avoided a trip to the emergency room because a timely prescription of oral antibiotics quickly resolved Miriam's confusion and altered mental status.

She had presented the same exact way, or with poor appetite, increased agitation, insomnia, and a host of other symptoms, many other times. By asking Miriam's doctor to send a home nurse for blood draws, administration of intravenous fluids or antibiotics, and even an ultrasound once to rule out a blood clot, we had avoided many unnecessary emergency room visits.

When a patient's baseline health can be variable, such as in the case of dementia patients, it can be exceptionally challenging to determine the appropriate course of treatment. The recommendations would have been very different if Miriam's PCP had reviewed the test results because he was familiar with her fluctuating symptoms.

Miriam had a long-standing history of chronic issues leading to low blood sodium levels and abnormal urine tests, which her specialists and general practitioners knew didn't always warrant aggressive treatment or hospital admissions. Unfortunately, the new covering doctor, despite having access to Miriam's records, couldn't thoroughly review years of medical history in a short time frame. However, after a brief call from me and reassurance that most of these issues were chronic and her confusion wasn't unusual, the doctor was relieved to recommend continued care at home with close follow-up.

Doctors require coverage for unexpected illness or during vacations. It's difficult for a new doctor to become familiar with years of patient data and records. Add that to the ever-growing concern of practicing defensive medicine in an era when legal action against doctors is commonplace, and you can quickly understand why doctors would see a visit to the emergency room for further evaluation as one of the safest options to protect the patient and themselves.

Miriam's case illustrates the importance of active healthcare involvement and advocacy. Open communication with her medical team prevented an unnecessary trip to the hospital, highlighting the value of a strong patient-provider relationship. This situation also emphasizes the complexities of healthcare decisions, especially for patients with fluctuating symptoms like dementia.

When you experience new and worrisome symptoms, you might think about heading straight to the ER. However, it might come as a surprise that most ER visits aren't real emergencies. Each year, there are nearly 140 million trips to the ER, but only 13% of these result in admissions.[1] When you consider cost, an ER visit can be 12 times more expensive than seeing a PCP and 10 times more costly than an urgent care facility. So, it's a good idea to consider if a visit to the ER is really needed.[2]

PRACTICAL TIPS TO MINIMIZE UNNECESSARY ER VISITS

1. Seek Help Early: One of the most important factors is getting help early. If you have a cough that has been going on for a week, then develop shortness of breath the second week, please don't wait till the third week to ask for a doctor's help. Early intervention is crucial, and waiting until the last minute can have serious consequences.

2. Prioritize In-Person Visits: When hospitalization is a consideration, an in-person visit with your doctor can be highly valuable. Seeing them in person allows assessment of vital information, such as blood pressure, oxygenation status, heart rate, other physical exam findings, and possibly even diagnostics, such as an EKG or chest X-ray, which could provide critical information to help ease the decision-making regarding a hospital admission.

While seeing your primary doctor is ideal, a specialist who knows your medical history well can also be valuable, especially if your symptoms relate to their expertise.

3. Access a Provider Network: If you can't reach your primary doctor or specialist, another practitioner with access to your medical records is the next best step. This could be a doctor in the same clinic or medical group who can review your past notes, labs, and X-rays, and provide valuable insights.

4. Consider Urgent Care: If your preferred doctors are unavailable, urgent care is an option. Have accurate and up-to-date information to share with the urgent care staff. Having a concise summary of your medical history, medications, and allergies, as discussed in Chapter 3, can be helpful.

5. Explore Home-Based Care: If transportation and access are challenges, explore resources and services that offer home visits by doctors and nurses. Keep comprehensive records of your medical history, medication dosages, and allergies, and always have your advance directive and health proxy's information readily available.

These steps can help you navigate healthcare decisions and potentially avoid unnecessary emergency room visits.

TELEMEDICINE: A DOUBLE-EDGED SWORD

Over the last few years, telemedicine and virtual appointments have exploded in popularity. Telemedicine has become popular due to its potential benefits, such as increased access to care for patients in rural locations; those facing challenges with transportation, childcare, or time off work; and seniors with mobility concerns. It also reduces infection risks, such as for post-op patients and those who are immunosuppressed.

However, while a video camera allows doctors to see you, it falls short of replacing an actual physical exam. When critical decisions need to be made about hospital admissions, not being able to fully examine and observe the patient presents a significant disadvantage. Furthermore, telemedicine may reduce access to care for certain patients, such as seniors who face Internet connectivity challenges, language barriers, or technological limitations. In essence, whenever feasible, an in-person visit remains the preferred option.

In an interesting study, researchers reviewed over 2,000 clinic patients to compare telemedicine to in-person visits.[3] They found that some types of doctors, like psychiatrists, radiologists, and hematologists/oncologists, got the best scores on making accurate diagnoses through telemedicine, while ear-nose-throat specialists, rheumatologists, internists, and pediatricians (who are often PCPs) had lower accuracy rates in telemedicine diagnoses. This isn't surprising, since the latter list of doctors relies more on physical examinations to help with accurate diagnosis. Additionally, researchers discovered that as people got older, the accuracy of telemedicine diagnoses went down. So, while telemedicine may be great for some things, it should not be our automatic choice for all appointments.

WHEN THE ER IS INEVITABLE

Maybe your illness came on suddenly, or you couldn't reach your doctor and have severe and concerning symptoms. In the previous chapters, we discussed the importance of having a well-thought-out medical emergency plan, so by now, you've diligently assembled your team of expert doctors. You've maintained thorough records of your relevant medical history. Most importantly, you have a copy of your advance directives, the contact information for your healthcare proxy, and the phone numbers of your closest relatives at hand. These proactive steps have already placed you in a better position than many others. You should feel very proud of your efforts to ensure your safety. Now, let's focus on the specifics of ER care.

Certain conditions necessitate immediate evaluation. The list below highlights *some* of these red flag conditions, which should never be ignored.

1. **Severe Injuries:** Head injuries, fractures, dislocations, or severe bleeding.
2. **Severe Allergic Reactions:** Difficulty breathing, swelling of the face or throat, or severe itching, which could indicate anaphylaxis.
3. **Severe Abdominal Pain:** Especially if it's sudden and intense, as it could indicate a ruptured organ or other serious abdominal issues.
4. **High Fever:** Particularly in infants, young children, or the elderly. Concerning signs and symptoms include high fever, chills, severe pain, severe headache, confusion, stiff neck, or rash.
5. **Chest Pain:** Especially if it's severe or associated with shortness of breath, sweating, or radiating pain down the arm, which could indicate a potential heart attack.
6. **Difficulty Breathing:** Especially if it's sudden and severe, as it could indicate a respiratory emergency.
7. **Severe Headache:** Especially if it's sudden and accompanied by neurological symptoms like weakness, confusion, or difficulty speaking, as it could indicate a stroke or other serious brain issues.
8. **Seizures:** Particularly if they are new or prolonged, or if multiple episodes occur.

9. **Loss of Consciousness:** Especially if it lasts for more than a few seconds or is accompanied by confusion or seizures.
10. **Severe Dehydration:** Especially if it's accompanied by confusion, rapid breathing, or a weak and rapid pulse.
11. **Poisoning:** Suspected ingestion of toxic substances or exposure to hazardous chemicals.
12. **Suicidal Thoughts or Self-Harm:** Immediate mental health crisis requiring emergency psychiatric care.

It's important to note that the urgency of seeking medical care can vary depending on severity and circumstances. However, if any of these symptoms occur, they should be taken seriously and evaluated promptly. In a true emergency, don't hesitate to call 911 or go to your nearest ER. For less urgent situations or when unsure, discuss with your PCP. They can help you determine whether an ER visit is warranted.

IMPROVING EFFICIENCY AND COMFORT

Having accompanied my family members to the hospital many times, I've developed strategies to enhance the efficiency of our ER visits. I contact nearby emergency departments to inquire about current wait times. In some cases, I had the luxury of choosing between two or three facilities of comparable quality, and my decision often came down to the shortest wait time—much like choosing a restaurant.

I also take into account the timing of our visits. Recognizing that many hospitals undergo nursing shift changes in the early morning and evening, commonly at 7:00 a.m. and 7:00 p.m., and often have reduced weekend staffing, I aim to make an ER visit during the day or midweek whenever possible. This helps minimize delays and wait times, which is crucial when someone isn't feeling their best.

Please note that these efficiency strategies apply *only* when symptoms are milder or progress gradually. In a serious emergency requiring immediate medical attention, seeking help without delay is paramount.

TRIAGE IN THE ER: PRIORITIZING CARE

Shortly after arriving at the ER, skilled nurses will assess your symptoms, check vital signs (like heart rate, blood pressure, and breathing rate), and assess the severity of your condition. Priority is given to patients with the red flag symptoms listed above, as they require immediate attention. Patients with milder symptoms and stable vitals may experience longer wait times. When you're seen, an ER physician will assess you to determine the care you need next. There are a few likely scenarios:

1. **Return Home:** If you have mild symptoms that can be managed with medications or simple interventions, you're treated and advised to follow up with your regular doctor.
2. **Observation Unit Stay:** You may require a brief stay (twenty-four to forty-eight hours) for stabilization and focused treatment prior to discharge. Common reasons include chest pain, stabilization after a procedure, blood transfusions, and possible transient conditions, such as a brief episode of fainting or ministroke.
3. **Hospital Admission:** If you have a more complex case, you may be admitted for more extensive testing, monitoring, and treatment. Typical medical or surgical

units cater to a wide range of medical issues, such as pneumonia, diabetes, minor surgeries, fractures, and other non-life-threatening conditions.

4. **Intensive Care Unit (ICU):** You'll typically be transferred to the ICU if you have a severe or life-threatening medical condition that requires closer monitoring, such as a severe infection, heart problem, severe breathing issues, major surgery, trauma, or organ failure. The ICU provides constant supervision by a highly trained medical team, advanced equipment, and immediate access to lifesaving interventions.

The Escalating Crisis of ER Wait Times

Pre-pandemic, the average ER wait times were estimated to be between 1 and 2.5 hours in various states, but this has worsened considerably in recent years. Despite fewer COVID hospitalizations, the crisis of post-pandemic access to care and lengthy ER waits persists nationwide. Hospitals are struggling with increased patient volumes, deferred care backlogs, and staffing shortages, leading to wait times of up to 16 hours before a patient is seen by a physician. This overcrowding is exacerbated by the uninsured who rely on emergency rooms for primary care due to limited access to regular healthcare providers. These conditions are reflective of widespread systemic healthcare challenges and may not see easy solutions anytime soon.[4]

DIRECT ADMISSION

Before we delve into strategies for navigating the ER, let's discuss an important process known as direct admissions.

Direct hospital admission, in simple terms, means you go directly to the hospital for medical care without first visiting the ER. This option is possible only if you've already been under the care of a doctor who knows your medical history and case well. That doctor sets into motion the steps that lead to direct admission. If they have admitting privileges to a specific hospital, you might receive care directly from your own doctor. However, if your doctor doesn't admit and care for patients personally, they can call the hospital's admitting doctors and explain why they want you admitted directly. While this option is usually suggested by the doctor and not the patient, it never hurts to ask.

Direct admission can save you time and ensure you receive the most efficient and coordinated care for your needs. More importantly, this process can also significantly decrease the stress associated with waiting in the ER. Instead of dealing with a hectic environment, you can start your treatment in a quieter and more controlled hospital setting. However, the decision to pursue direct admission depends on various factors, including your medical needs, your doctor's recommendations, bed availability, and the hospital's policies. In cases of emergencies, the ER remains the appropriate choice for immediate and critical care.

ER TIP #1: ADVOCATE

When your loved one is in the ER—and particularly if they're too ill or confused to communicate important information to the doctors—it's highly advisable for you or someone familiar with the patient to remain with them for as long as possible, ideally until the decision regarding admission is reached. Your role as a patient advocate is crucial because you can provide a clear, concise, and efficient description of the events leading up to the emergency visit. The more precise the information you provide, the more valuable it will be for the doctor.

ERs are often fast-paced environments where healthcare professionals are caring for many seriously ill patients. Often, patients arrive without comprehensive medical records, adding to the challenges doctors face as they work hard to recommend appropriate diagnostic tests and treatments in a timely fashion.

During one of my father's episodes of chest pain, a potentially dangerous symptom for someone with his cardiac history, I had to take him to an unfamiliar ER without access to his medical records. After what felt like an agonizingly long wait, a visibly rushed and somewhat disheveled ER doctor finally approached us. I hurriedly presented him with the highlights of Dad's medical history, which included many heart-related complications and hospitalizations. Yet the doctor dismissed the chest pain as unrelated to his heart and suggested sending him home. As we discussed and debated the situation, the doctor eventually revealed that he was finishing his shift and had hoped to discharge my father so his bed would be available for the next shift. This revelation left both my father and me frustrated, as we'd anticipated a more thorough examination based on his cardiac history. I strongly believe that access to my father's comprehensive medical records could have led to a different course of action by the doctor. In our case, my ability to highlight his history and complications, which indicated higher risk, played a crucial role. Only by advocating for my dad and delving into his detailed medical history were we able to capture the doctor's attention, resulting in additional testing before discharge.

It's commonly known, at least to most physicians, that nearly 80% of diagnoses are made based on a patient's medical history alone. Depending on the study, the physical exam may contribute another 10% to 12% in helping with the correct diagnosis.[5] While medical technology has advanced, history and examination skills remain fundamental in clinical practice. These days, however, doctors often work in rushed environments and may lack the time needed for thorough record reviews, history taking, or detailed exams. This situation can lead to missed diagnoses or unnecessary tests. Therefore, being present and proactive in advocating is crucial for ensuring the best care.

ER TIP #2: GET YOUR PRIMARY CARE DOCTOR INVOLVED

In my own practice, I made it a priority to contact the ER doctor whenever my patients needed emergency care. Sharing the patient's medical history and highlighting the important stuff ensured more efficient care. While the ER doctor still had to sift through digital records, labs, old X-rays, CT scans, or MRIs, our direct communication was a game changer.

This kind of direct communication is invaluable for the busy ER doctor who's unfamiliar with the patient and has limited time to make major decisions. It often leads to faster orders for the right tests, cultures, antibiotics, or even earlier involvement of specialists.

All this to say, if you can have your regular doctors communicating with the ER physicians, it can really help!

ER TIP #3: COMMUNICATE WITH CLARITY AND PATIENCE

In a busy ER, you may encounter many healthcare providers—nurses, students, social workers, administrators, residents, and various doctors—especially if your case is complex. It's incredibly helpful to ask questions and request the person's contact or business card when they visit you. Knowing their name and role ensures that you're sharing the right information with the right people.

Get ready for the possibility that you'll need to tell your medical story, list your medications, and describe your symptoms multiple times. Even though it might seem like you're repeating yourself, being patient and answering these questions can help improve your care. Busy doctors may not always have a lot of time to get a comprehensive history, so different practitioners asking in-depth questions can only positively impact your care.

Consider this: the first person you spoke with might not have gathered all the necessary details. Imagine a scenario where the initial doctor missed asking details about your updated medication list or allergies and their severity, leading to an incomplete or inaccurate medical record. Or think about a treatment or surgery that was omitted but could be vital to your case. Any staff member who's taking the time to gather a more thorough history should be appreciated.

These issues can become even more challenging with elderly or confused patients. Initial interviews could involve caregivers or family members. But if they're not present throughout the ER stay, all subsequent healthcare providers have to rely on that initial information. To prevent misunderstandings and improve care decisions, it's crucial to have someone stay with the patient or ensure that staff knows how to reach family or caregivers.

TEACHABLE POINTS

1. **Early Intervention Matters:** Seek help early in the course of your illness. Don't wait until symptoms worsen significantly before reaching out to a healthcare provider.
2. **Patient-Provider Relationship:** A strong patient-provider relationship is crucial. It can prevent unnecessary hospitalizations and ensure you receive appropriate medical care.
3. **Explore Home-Based Care:** If transportation or access is challenging, investigate resources and services that offer home visits by doctors and nurses.
4. **Telemedicine's Popularity:** Telemedicine has gained popularity in recent years for its convenience and potential benefits, especially for patients in rural areas or with mobility issues. However, it can't always replace an in-person physical examination when critical decisions about hospital admissions are required.
5. **Evaluate Symptom Severity:** Recognize that many ER visits are not true emergencies and can be more costly; consider using primary care, specialists, or urgent care services early on to avoid unnecessary trips to the ER.
6. **Red Flag Symptoms:** Be aware of red flag symptoms that require immediate evaluation at the ER, such

as severe injuries, allergic reactions, chest pain, or difficulty breathing. Delay in evaluation can have adverse consequences. Call 911 or go to the nearest ER in such cases.

7. **Direct Admission:** Understand what direct admission is and how it can be beneficial in specific situations, potentially bypassing the ER.

8. **Patient Advocacy:** Recognize the crucial role of patient advocacy in the ER, particularly for individuals who may not effectively communicate their medical history.

CHAPTER 5

ENSURING A SAFE OVERNIGHT HOSPITAL STAY

As you transition from the emergency room (ER) to a hospital stay, the ER physician recommends admission based on your specific medical needs. Your journey might lead you to specialized units tailored to your condition, such as the cardiac care unit (CCU), intensive care unit (ICU), orthopedic unit, or a general medical/surgical floor. For most of my career, once admission was decided, there would be an efficient transfer from the ER to a hospital unit and a smooth handoff to a new medical team. Nowadays, the experience of hospital admission can be significantly different.

These days, and for possibly years to come, as hospitals continue to be overcrowded from deferred care during the pandemic, high burnout rates, and serious staff shortages, patients are staying in the emergency room longer and longer even after admission.[1]

What has taken the place of a prompt transfer out of an ER bed to a private hospital room has been replaced

with longer "boarding" times in the emergency room—
awaiting an inpatient hospital bed. To alleviate this crisis,
patients are being accommodated in emergency room
hallways and lobbies and the use of areas not typically
meant for overnight stays. Unfortunately, this is not
typically just for a few hours, but in fact for many days or
even the entire duration of their stays.

The concern here is far more than just inconvenience
to patients and their families. The Joint Commission, a
body that accredits and certifies healthcare organizations,
ensuring safe and effective care, has identified boarding
as a patient safety risk that should not exceed four hours![2]
However, it's become common to exceed this time frame,
which can lead to serious consequences such as medical
errors, violations of privacy, and even a greater likelihood
of death.[3]

These changes emphasize the need for patients and their
families to remain vigilant and proactive during their ER
stays and after admission. Navigating this new landscape
requires awareness and a strong voice in advocating for
the best possible care.

WATCH OUT FOR GAPS IN CARE

If you're admitted to the hospital overnight, either after
being seen by the ER doctor or through a direct admission,
it's important to be aware of potential gaps in care that
can occur during transitions in your care. Typically, your
care will shift to another medical team responsible for
inpatient care. However, it's important to note that
staffing levels, especially for in-hospital physicians, can
vary widely among hospitals. Many facilities have fewer
doctors available during nighttime hours compared to

daytime. I've also observed that the nighttime nursing staff may consist of nurses who are relatively new in their careers or have recently completed their training. Let me emphasize that this observation may not be applicable to all hospitals or all-night nursing staff and is just an observation from friends and family who work as nurses. Regardless, these staffing issues can impact timely care, especially for vulnerable patients, such as the elderly, who frequently experience confusion and delirium during hospitalization. In such cases, having a family member stay until the new team of admitting doctors has taken over care can make a big difference.

I recall an unfortunate night when a relative was directly admitted to the hospital from the kidney specialist's office. This admission followed a clinic visit where my relative was found to urgently need hospitalization and dialysis due to excessive fluid in their lungs. They were in considerable discomfort, with severely swollen legs and extreme difficulty breathing. Due to the direct admission by the doctor, we were able to bypass the chaos of the ER and make our way to the hospital room rather smoothly.

However, a crucial handoff to the inpatient doctor, or hospitalist, seemed to slip through the cracks. While our outpatient specialist had arranged for the hospital room and initiated basic orders for diet, a few medications, and urgent dialysis, he had forgotten to include orders for the vital blood pressure medication required at night. Consequently, our nurse was left without orders for these critical medications, leaving my relative with blood pressures exceeding 190 for several hours. This level is extremely high and dangerous. Left untreated, it can put a patient at risk of stroke, heart attack and much more.

You can probably understand my frustration in this situation. We were in a hospital, facing an urgent medical issue, and couldn't get the necessary medications. Despite the nurse's persistent attempts to contact the clinic doctor or other staff who could provide guidance, she was unable to secure the appropriate medication. It still puzzles me why none of the doctors ever responded to her calls. The only solution was to get the medications from home. Just imagine what might have happened if we'd left promptly after the late-evening admission, assuming everything would proceed smoothly. Most likely, my relative wouldn't have been in a state to be aware of the elevated blood pressure, and they certainly weren't in a position to advocate for themselves.

KNOW YOUR INPATIENT (HOSPITAL) PROVIDERS

Upon admission to the hospital, you'll most likely encounter a variety of new faces, including doctors, nurses, students, physical therapists, occupational therapists, social workers, nutritionists, volunteers, and chaplains.

HOSPITALIST

In most cases, hospitalists take the lead in your care. They're a specialized group of doctors primarily dedicated to caring for hospitalized patients. The term *hospitalist* was first used in 1996 to describe this medical specialty, which typically includes internal medicine or family medicine doctors. In nonteaching hospitals, there's usually one hospitalist physician responsible for your care. In an attempt to maintain continuity, many hospitals try to have hospitalists work a number of consecutive days or weeks in a row. Over the years, the most common schedule I've seen is a week on followed by a week off. In some hospitals, I've seen this extended to two weeks of continuous work before getting time off. The weekends may or may not be covered by the same hospitalist.

In teaching or academic hospitals, remembering the hierarchy, roles, and titles of different doctors can be a lot more complex. In this setting, the most senior physician on any team is referred to as the "medical attending." The medical attending, commonly shortened to "attending," can be a hospitalist, surgeon, or other specialist. Depending on varying protocols in different teaching facilities, you may be admitted from the ER to a specialty team (e.g., one that's led by a cardiologist attending) or a general medicine team (led by a hospitalist medical attending). In a teaching hospital, there continues to be one lead hospitalist. The main difference between teaching and nonteaching facilities is that in a teaching hospital, each hospitalist or attending often works alongside several more junior doctors in training.

For example, a patient may be admitted to a hospitalist team that's led by one hospitalist medical attending and includes four to six other junior doctors with varying years of clinical experience. Now imagine the patient also requires the care of additional hospital specialists, like heart specialists or surgeons, and that each specialty team also contains an additional two to four more junior doctors. It's not uncommon for a patient, especially the more complex ones, to see somewhere between 10 and 20 doctors in any one day in a teaching hospital.

Regardless of the number of doctors and staff, it's important to remember that hospitalists serve as your primary medical providers during your hospital stay. They make decisions about your admission from the ER, oversee your care, consult with specialists as necessary, order tests and treatments, and coordinate with your primary outpatient providers when required. As you approach discharge, the hospitalist, with assistance from discharge planners or case managers, handles paperwork, medications, follow-up appointments, and home equipment. Given their pivotal role in your care, it's crucial that you and your family maintain regular communication with the hospitalist.

While being cared for by a hospitalist during a hospitalization is the most common scenario, your care may be directly managed by surgical teams or other specialty teams, such as cardiology, oncology, or orthopedics, especially in cases where there's one main health issue and not a multitude of complex problems. Examples of this include a patient without many medical problems who has a heart attack and is admitted directly to a cardiology team, or one with a hip fracture who's admitted directly to an orthopedic team.

The following list provides an overview of different healthcare providers in descending order of their training and expertise in the complex hospital setting.

PHYSICIAN ROLES (TEACHING AND NONTEACHING HOSPITALS)

MEDICAL ATTENDING/HOSPITALIST
— Undergraduate Education: 4-year bachelor's degree
— Medical School: 4-year Doctor of Medicine degree
— Residency: 3 to 7 years of completed postgraduate training
— Clinical Training Hours: Varies, approximately 12,000 to 16,000 hours

— Duties: The term medical attending, or just attending, refers to the most senior physician in a teaching hospital. In nonteaching hospitals, all doctors are essentially equivalent to an attending because there are no other junior doctors caring for patients. These highly trained doctors have completed their medical education and training, are fully licensed, and bear ultimate responsibility for patient care decisions. They have the authority to make final decisions on patient treatments and may serve as mentors, educators, and leaders in the department or hospital.

PHYSICIAN ROLES (TYPICALLY TEACHING HOSPITALS ONLY)

FELLOW

— Undergraduate Education: 4-year bachelor's degree
— Medical School: 4-year Doctor of Medicine degree
— Residency: 3 to 7 years post–medical school
— Fellowship: 1 to 3 years post-residency
— Duties: These physicians have graduated from medical school and completed a general residency program, such as internal medicine or general surgery. They're now pursuing specialized training in a specific subspecialty, such as cardiology, infectious disease, or oncology. Fellows typically possess more clinical experience and expertise within their chosen subspecialty compared to residents. They often take on supervisory roles for residents within their subspecialty, engage in patient care and procedures, and contribute to research activities. Fellows work closely with attending physicians and may participate in teaching and mentoring roles for residents and medical students.

MEDICAL RESIDENT
— Undergraduate Education: 4-year bachelor's degree
— Medical School: 4-year Doctor of Medicine degree
— Residency: 2 to 7 years post–medical school
— Duties: These physicians have graduated from medical school and are currently undergoing postgraduate training, known as residency, within a general field, like internal medicine or surgery. They provide direct patient care, perform medical procedures, and are supervised by attending physicians. They participate in educational, research, and clinical activities as part of their training. They also mentor interns and medical students.

MEDICAL INTERN
— Undergraduate Education: 4-year bachelor's degree
— Medical School: 4-year Doctor of Medicine degree
— Residency: First year of residency post–medical school
— Duties: Physicians who are recent medical school graduates typically start a three-to-seven-year residency. The first year, called "internship," is where they primarily focus on hands-on patient care and evaluations, working under the supervision of residents and attendings. While they may have the ability to write orders and provide initial treatment, their decisions are often subject to review and approval by more senior physicians.

MEDICAL STUDENT
— Undergraduate Education: 4-year bachelor's degree
— Medical School: Hospital rotations or training typically start in the third and fourth year
— Duties: As the most junior members of the physician team, students transition from textbook learning in the first two years to practical hands-on training.

Since they're responsible for only a few patients, they often provide focused attention and time. They may even see patients before the rest of the medical team or with the help of more senior physicians. However, medical students don't possess the experience, seniority, or authority to make final treatment decisions independently.

NONPHYSICIAN ROLES

PHYSICIAN ASSISTANT (PA)

— Undergraduate Education: Typically 4-year bachelor's degree
— Physician Assistant Program: 2 years
— Residency: Optional 1 to 2 years
— Clinical Training Hours: 1,000 to 2,000 hours (varies state to state)
— Duties: PAs can work in various specialties, providing diagnostic, therapeutic, and preventive healthcare services, often working alongside physicians

NURSE PRACTITIONERS (NP): MSN (MASTER OF SCIENCE IN NURSING) OR DNP (DOCTORATE IN NURSING)

— Undergraduate Education: Typically 4 years for Bachelor of Science in Nursing
— Advanced Nursing Education: 2 to 4 years post-bachelor's (can be online)
— Residency: Optional
— Clinical Training Hours: 500 to 1,000 (varies state to state)
— Duties: NPs are advanced practice nurses who have completed training beyond the requirements for a registered nurse (RN) license. An MSN-NP program provides specialized training in a particular patient

population or area of practice, such as family nurse practitioner (FNP). Some obtain additional training as DNP-NPs, which is the highest level of nursing education and training. DNPs typically take on leadership roles and provide advanced care to patients.

Both MSN-NPs and DNP-NPs can work as advanced practice nurses, assess patients, diagnose conditions, create treatment plans, and prescribe medications. The extent to which NPs can practice independently varies from state to state due to differences in state regulations and scope-of-practice laws.

REGISTERED NURSE (RN)
— Undergraduate Education (or Post–High School Education): Typically 2 to 4 years
— Residency: Optional
— Clinical Training Hours: 500 to 800 (varies state to state)
— Duties: Most commonly, this is the provider you'll interact the most with during a hospitalization. They conduct initial patient assessments, follow care plans, administer medications, educate patients and families, and coordinate care. It's important to note that RNs cannot diagnose or prescribe medication.

CERTIFIED NURSING ASSISTANT (CNA)
— Total Post–High School Education: 1 to 4 months (varies state to state)
— Duties: Another provider you may see frequently in the hospital, a CNA plays a critical role in patient care, including taking vital signs, such as blood pressure; assisting with eating, bathing, and dressing; transporting patients for tests; maintaining cleanliness

in patient rooms; responding to patient calls; repositioning or moving patients; restocking supplies; and documenting patient information. They also serve as intermediaries between patients and nursing staff, relaying patient concerns or complaints to the nursing team for appropriate triage and care coordination.

ANESTHESIA CARE: KNOW YOUR PROVIDER

When undergoing surgery, your anesthesia care may be managed by either an anesthesiologist or a Certified Registered Nurse Anesthetist (CRNA). Anesthesiologists are medical doctors with extensive training in anesthesia, pain management, and critical care. CRNAs are advanced practice nurses who, after obtaining a nursing degree and critical care experience, complete a graduate program in nurse anesthesia.

ANESTHESIOLOGIST

— Bachelor's Degree: Typically 4 years
— Medical School (MD or DO): 4 years
— Residency in Anesthesiology: 4 years or more
— Total Education & Training: Anesthesiologists complete a rigorous clinical residency program, which includes extensive hands-on training in anesthesia care. The education and training can take 12-15 years.

CERTIFIED REGISTERED NURSE ANESTHETIST (CRNA)

— Bachelor of Science in Nursing (BSN) or equivalent: Typically 4 years
— Critical Care Experience (After obtaining Registered Nurse License): 1 year or more
— Doctoral Degree: Typically 3 years
— Total Education & Training: CRNAs must complete extensive clinical training during their nurse anesthesia

program. The education and training can take 8-10 years.

Currently, in over 24 states, CRNAs can practice independently and without requirement for physician supervision, a change that has increased access to anesthesia care, especially in rural hospitals where they represent more than 80% of the anesthesia providers.[4] They are also the primary providers of anesthesia in nearly half of all rural hospitals for obstetric care.[5] While both healthcare providers play vital roles in patient care, you need to understand your right to be informed and ask questions about your anesthesia provider. In rural settings or situations with limited providers, options may be limited. However, in elective or less urgent procedures, you can ask about who is administering your anesthesia, and there may be instances where different options are available.

PARTNERING WITH YOUR PROVIDERS

To reiterate, the point of going through this lengthy list of physician and nonphysician tiers of training is mostly to build greater awareness around whom the patient is speaking with and getting their information from. It's good to realize that some of the information obtained from more junior providers on the team may need to be confirmed or discussed in greater detail with a more senior resident or attending if you or your family have a concern.

I recall many situations when I asked a hospitalized family member for their doctors' names and got only blank stares. Furthermore, they were always confused about whom they thought they were talking to. Sometimes they mistakenly thought a younger attending was actually an intern or resident. In other situations, they mistakenly thought a nurse or physician assistant was the attending.

Knowing whom you're talking to sets up realistic expectations that can prevent a lot of frustration during your hospital stay. It's fairly important (and often challenging) to keep track of all the doctors and specialists who visit you in the hospital. As mentioned, it's helpful to ask for each person's business card at the time of the visit. And don't hesitate to ask people what their role in your care may be.

The more involved and engaged you or your family are—of course, without excessively disrupting the staff—the more knowledgeable you'll be about your care. It helps you get the full picture and makes decisions a bit easier. I believe most doctors appreciate when patients and families are involved and interested in their health. It's all about teaming up with your healthcare team for the best results.

PROVIDER CHALLENGES AND PATIENT ADVOCACY

CHALLENGES TO NURSING CARE

Another important aspect of safety and quality of care has to do with how much attention you get from each of your providers. In any health setting, facilities must be mindful of maintaining optimal nurse-to-patient ratios to ensure sicker patients get the time and attention they need. Lots of research shows that the number of nurses on duty is a big deal. For example, studies suggest that having more registered nurses around was linked to fewer patient deaths, cardiac arrests, hospital infections,[6] falls,[7] and even reduced medication errors.[8] Another interesting study directly links hospital nurse staffing levels to patient mortality.[9] The study examined whether surgical mortality is lower in hospitals where nurses care for fewer patients. The study found the following:

- Each additional patient per nurse was associated with a 7% increase in the likelihood of dying within 30 days of admission.
- An increase in the nurse's patient workload from 4 patients to 6 led to a 14% increase in patient deaths.

Interestingly, rules and regulations about what are considered optimal nurse-to-patient ratios can vary depending on where you are in the US. However, California stands out as the only state that has specific rules for different hospital units. There, the mandated nurse-to-patient ratios are:

- ER with a trauma patient—1:1
- ICU—1:2
- ER (not trauma)—1:4
- Medical/surgical units—1:5
- Psychiatry units—1:6

These ratios serve as guidelines to ensure patients receive the appropriate level of care depending on their condition. However, be aware that some hospitals may attempt to manipulate these ratios. They may attempt to place sicker patients who require higher monitoring on a regular medical/surgical unit—for example, putting an unstable diabetic patient or a patient with fluctuating neurologic status after a recent brain hemorrhage in a unit that's not meant for these unstable patients. This practice makes it appear the hospital is maintaining the recommended ratio on paper, but in reality, it places undue stress on nursing staff as they care for patients with higher needs in units not designed for such cases.

So, what can you do to assess if the hospital or unit you're in is being managed in the best way possible? Here are some suggestions:

1. **Ask Your Nurse:** Learn about the number of patients they're responsible for and compare it to the recommended ratios above. This can help you gauge workload and prompt you to advocate for your care.
2. **Stay Informed:** Stay updated on news about the hospital. Layoffs or job cuts can affect whether the hospital meets the recommended staffing levels.
3. **Ask about Support Staff:** Find out if the hospital has specialized staff for tasks like EKGs and blood draws. This ensures that nurses can focus on patient care rather than additional responsibilities.
4. **Speak Up:** If you have concerns about staffing levels and care, don't hesitate to voice them. Your health and safety are paramount.
5. **Obtain Additional Support:** If you sense that the nursing staff are carrying a heavy load of patients, you might want to consider having a loved one stay with you in the hospital to provide additional support. Alternatively, hiring a caregiver can ensure you receive the attention and care you need.

Since recommended nurse-to-patient ratios can impact your safety, consider comparing different hospitals on these factors, as discussed in the "Starting Your Research" section of Chapter 1. Your well-being is a top priority during your hospital stay, and being proactive can make a significant difference in the quality of care you receive.

CHALLENGES TO PHYSICIAN CARE

An increasing number of studies shows that regardless of the specialty, more doctors are spending more of their time looking at electronic health records than interacting with patients. One study assessing productivity in a community hospital ER found that 43% of the doctor's time was spent on data entry, 28% on direct patient care, 12% on reviewing test results and records, 13% on discussion with colleagues, and 4% on other activities.[10] That means in a 10-hour ER shift, the doctor spends 7.2 hours on tasks other than direct patient care, leaving only 2.8 hours for actual patient interaction. Assuming a typical ER doctor evaluates somewhere between 13 and 20 patients per shift,[11] that translates into 8 to 12 minutes per patient, which isn't much time.

Studies looking at how doctors in training manage their time show much of the same trend. Since the 1980s, increasing pressures on training programs to limit long work hours and increasing demands for documentation in complex electronic health records have resulted in doctors in training spending less time with patients and more time with their computers. One study from 2019 showed that, in a 24-hour period, 66% of that time was spent in indirect patient care,[12] which essentially translated into interactions with the patient's medical record (reviewing medical records or recording their notes, ordering labs and tests, etc.), while 13% of the time was focused on direct patient care (including patient evaluation, exam, communication, and family communication). The rest consisted of educational activities.

These statistics highlight the importance of making efficient use of your time when interacting with doctors. Communicate any concerns or change in symptoms clearly and promptly. These days, I'm happily surprised when I see that my hospital patients (or their families) have already logged in to their patient portal to check their labs before I've even had my daily visits. Generally, whether you're in the hospital or an outpatient setting, I think it is a good idea to be familiar with your lab or imaging abnormalities. Engaged patients are more likely to ask questions that could be very important to their care.

Among my own family members—most of whom aren't native speakers—I've seen a bit of anxiety and maybe even ambivalence around asking too many questions. Yet research indicates that when patients actively take part in their care, it tends to make healthcare better. This means that the quality of care and safety improve, there are fewer mistakes, and care becomes more efficient. When patients are included as part of the healthcare team, both patients and doctors are happier, and the results are generally better.[13]

IMPROVING COMMUNICATIONS

In light of some of the challenges discussed above, it's worth addressing some basics about family communications. Typically, when you or a family member need to get in touch with a doctor, it's best to have one designated person in charge. Preferably, this would be the chosen healthcare proxy, who can communicate important information to the rest of the family. Getting a doctor on the phone for updates or questions can be challenging enough, much less expecting that doctor to call multiple family members. While it's common for many hospital physicians to see their patients from early morning to midday, anytime is fair game. If you're planning on physically being in the hospital to meet a family member's doctor, it may be helpful to ask the nurse what time a particular team or doctor typically rounds, or visits, their patients. Having caregivers or family members present early in the day to ask questions, get updates, or express concerns is more likely to make the communication process efficient and useful.

If the designated family member or healthcare proxy can't be there for meetings with the clinical team, give the hospital staff the contact number of *one* person who will be the point person for communications.

ENHANCING COMFORT IN THE HOSPITAL

There are other considerations to note during a hospital admission that will make life just a little easier. These include:

1. **Safeguard Personal Belongings:** Safely store or transfer valuable personal belongings home right after admission. I've seen a lot of missing dentures, hearing aids, canes, walkers, etc. over the years. Losing these important personal items is not only a cost issue but also leads to an increase in delirium and confusion, especially in the elderly, who need these personal devices for optimal functioning.
2. **Stay with Patients Who Need Help:** Have family or caregivers stay overnight with very young, elderly, confused, or disabled patients who may not be able to ask for help. I've seen relatives take turns, each covering a different shift so their loved ones are never or rarely alone. It's best to check with nursing or hospital staff about visiting hours and policies.

3. **Prioritize Restful Sleep:** Ask the physician and hospital care team if frequent overnight or early morning blood draws and testing can be minimized. Consider requesting a darker and quieter environment at night. If needed, request natural sleep aids, like melatonin, to improve sleep without causing excessive sedation or side effects. Let in natural sunlight (if possible) to regulate sleep patterns.

4. **Stay Cognitively Engaged:** Bring or ask for iPads, books, a radio, newspapers, and puzzles during a more prolonged stay. Some hospitals provide some of these options.

5. **Enhance Comfort:** Bring in pictures, personal blankets, drawings, flowers, and aromatherapy if allowed. Studies show that while being in nature has amazing healing powers, even viewing images or pictures of nature can be an incredible tool for activating the calming part of the nervous system.[14]

6. **Address Nutritional Needs:** Appetite, eating, and bowel changes are commonly impacted during a hospital stay, so be proactive about reporting issues or problems in any of these areas. If the food isn't to your liking, it may help to ask for a nutrition consultation during hospitalization to work out alternative strategies to ensure caloric needs are met. Don't be afraid to ask if you can have food brought in.

7. **Watch for Changes:** Blood clots in the legs (or even arms around placement of intravenous catheters), weakness and deconditioning, infections, cognitive decline in the elderly, falls, etc., are common. Be on the lookout for physical and mental changes, and report them to your doctors so prompt testing and treatment can be initiated to avoid life-threatening consequences.

8. **Consider Complementary Care:** If you're interested in integrative or complementary services, ask your hospital what services they offer. More and more prestigious universities and hospitals are offering acupuncture, Reiki, aromatherapy, and other integrative consultations while patients are hospitalized.

WHEN ALL ELSE FAILS: NAVIGATING CARE CONCERNS WITH PROFESSIONALISM

By now, I hope you've found some helpful tips for an improved hospital experience and enhanced communication with your healthcare provider. However, if you ever find that expressing your concerns hasn't resolved them, it's essential to know the next steps. I highly recommend approaching these steps calmly and objectively, as they require delicate navigation. It's important to understand that voicing dissatisfaction with your care or a specific provider may not always be met with open arms. How you communicate your concerns may significantly impact your relationship with your healthcare team. If you choose to request a second opinion or transfer to another hospital, there are no guarantees that you'll be successful. You may need to continue under the care of your initial providers. In such situations, maintain a composed, logical, and respectful manner while explaining why another facility or provider may better align with your health needs. This approach avoids blame and focuses on your preference for a better fit in your care. Here are some steps to consider:

1. **Use Open and Honest Communication:** If you haven't yet done so, start by communicating your concerns and dissatisfaction with the healthcare providers directly involved

in your care. Express your thoughts, feelings, and specific issues you've encountered. Ask questions about your condition, treatment plan, medications, or any procedures. Seek clarification if something is unclear to you.

2. **Request a Care Team (or Family) Meeting:** This may include doctors, nurses, specialists, and case managers. Discuss your concerns and collaboratively work on a plan to address them.

3. **Involve a Patient Advocate:** Many hospitals have patient advocates or patient liaison services. Reach out to them to express your concerns and request assistance in resolving issues.

4. **Familiarize Yourself with Hospital Policies:** Understand the hospital's policies and procedures, including your patient rights. Knowing your rights can empower you to advocate effectively for your care.

5. **Reach Out to Hospital Administration:** If your concerns persist, contact the hospital's administration or patient relations department to escalate your issues and seek resolution.

6. **Raise Ethical Concerns:** You can also request consultation with a hospital's ethics committee when you have concerns about the fairness of your medical care. This may include treatment decisions, such as whether to start or stop life-prolonging treatments, end-of-life care, conflicts of interest, patient rights, or complex ethical dilemmas. The ethics committee provides guidance and recommendations, ensuring that ethical principles are upheld in patient care. Procedures for involving the committee may vary by hospital.

7. **Consider a Hospital Transfer:** In extreme cases where your concerns remain unaddressed, you have the right to request a hospital transfer. Discuss this option with your care team or patient advocate. Keep in mind that transferring may involve significant challenges, such as finding a receiving hospital and physician. Advocating for yourself is crucial to ensure your well-being and safety during your hospital stay. Be proactive in seeking the care you need and deserve.

TEACHABLE POINTS

1. **Awareness of Care Transitions:** Be vigilant about potential gaps in care during transitions between medical teams when admitted to the hospital overnight. Staffing levels may vary, and having a family member present can be helpful, especially for vulnerable patients.

2. **Optimizing Healthcare Interactions:** Understand that providers may face challenges, such as high patient-to-provider ratios and administrative tasks that impact care. Recognize that staffing levels and efficient communication can significantly influence patient safety and the quality of care you receive.

3. **Effective Family Communication:** Designate one person to handle communications with the healthcare team. This streamlines information flow and helps ensure that important details are conveyed to the medical staff efficiently.

4. **Enhancing Patient Comfort:** Consider safe storage of personal belongings, having family or caregivers present, creating a comfortable environment, and exploring

integrative therapies to improve the overall hospital experience.

5. **Challenging Situations:** Start by expressing concerns with open, clear, and respectful communications to your healthcare providers. If issues persist, consider requesting a meeting with your care team, involving a patient advocate, or requesting an ethics consult or hospital transfer.

CHAPTER 6

RISKS OF A PROLONGED HOSPITAL STAY

A report from 2021 indicated the average length of stay (LOS) in US hospitals was 5.9 days. Interestingly, similar statistics across the globe indicate a big range, from New Zealand's average of 4.4 days to Japan's 16-day LOS.[1] While the term *prolonged hospitalization* doesn't have a single, universally agreed-upon definition, it's based on factors like the patient's medical condition and the purpose of their hospital stay. Different studies use varying definitions, typically ranging anywhere from 14 to 21 days.[2]

However, what's consistently evident across all these studies is that the longer someone stays in the hospital, the higher their chance of experiencing adverse events and complications. Although a patient and their family may want the longest possible stay for a more complete recovery, unnecessary and prolonged days in the hospital are more likely to lead to healthcare-associated infections, delirium and confusion, physical and cognitive decline (especially in the elderly), falls, and other complications.

Some of the reasons for a longer stay include a complicated course of illness, lack of safe placement options at time of discharge, reluctance of family members to take ill patients back home, limited availability of nursing homes or long-term facilities, and insurance issues, to name a few. In fact, a study focused on patients who had extended hospital stays found that one of the primary reasons for these prolonged stays was the challenge of arranging post-hospital care, such as placement in a rehabilitation center or returning home. This issue affected more than half of the patients and was the main cause of delay. This meant finding an appropriate place for discharge could cause, on average, more than eight days of delay, making this an important consideration in the early days of a hospital admission.[3]

While extended hospital stays can be problematic for patients of all ages, they can have a particularly significant and sometimes lasting impact on older individuals. Considering that a significant portion of hospitalized patients are 65 and older, it's crucial to prioritize this vulnerable group's well-being. In the sections that follow, we'll look at some of the potential areas to watch out for.

DELIRIUM AND COGNITIVE DECLINE

Delirium is a change in mental abilities that may result in altered thinking, confusion, lack of awareness, trouble focusing, trouble with speech, inability to recognize family members, anxiety, personality changes, fluctuating mood, etc. This process may develop over a short period of time from a few hours to gradually over a few days, and it's prevalent in 10% to 30% of hospitalized patients.[4] For those in the intensive care unit (ICU), the risk can rise to as much as 80%.[5] In my opinion, this is one of the most difficult areas of caring for hospitalized patients, and it carries risks that are underrecognized, costly, and dangerous. Admitting and caring for patients who are behaving differently than their baseline creates many challenges in the hospital, as most of the patients are new to the physicians who care for them there. Doctors are simply not familiar with these patients' baseline cognitive abilities.

Delirium can manifest in various ways, from increased agitation and confusion to quietness or sleepiness. These fluctuations can be problematic, especially for the elderly, as they increase the risk of falls and complications, like dislodging intravenous access or feeding tubes. To manage this, doctors may need to administer stronger medications, but these come with risks, including increased confusion and sedation.

Delirium can present commonly in elderly patients and represent a symptom of life-threatening medical conditions such as lack of oxygen, infections, organ failure, electrolyte abnormalities, and medication overdose, to name a few.[6] There are two types of delirium: *prevalent*, which is found at admission and often in those with dementia, and *incident*, which develops during the hospital stay. While incident delirium can lengthen hospital stays by up to eight days,[7] a recent study has found that having delirium of any kind doubles the likelihood of dying within 12 months after hospitalization.[8] This highlights the severe impact delirium has on the long-term health of older adults. Even months after a discharge, patients developing delirium in the hospital sometimes never bounce back to their prior baseline physical and cognitive abilities, leading to a significant risk of loss of independence.

Some factors that increase the risk of delirium may include advanced age, multiple medical problems and medications, baseline dementia, immobility, malnutrition, underlying kidney or liver disease, and vision or hearing impairment. One study showed that delirium frequently goes unnoticed or is misdiagnosed in a substantial proportion of older patients, often reaching up to 70% of cases.[9] A long list of medications, with a high risk of potential drug-drug interactions, can increase the precipitating factors leading up to delirium. Patients and caregivers need to be especially cautious with antidepressants, antihistamines, psychiatric medications, painkillers, and antiseizure medications, among others. In patients with underlying dementia or Alzheimer's, the prevalence of delirium could be substantial while hospitalized. Even in patients with no or minimal cognitive decline before hospitalization, an episode of delirium and confusion during hospitalization could translate into deficits that impact cognition over the long term.[10]

With the risk of delirium being so high in the elderly and the possibility of irreversible functional decline after hospitalization, it's important to minimize hospitalizations, shorten stays, and reduce disorientation during and after hospitalization. Below are some suggested strategies:

ORIENTATION

Assessment: Hospital staff can use monitoring tools and questions daily or even multiple times a day. Family and caregivers can also do informal assessments. Consider asking the patient orientation-related questions such as:

1. Which day of the week is it?
2. What's the date?
3. What's the month?

4. What season are we in?
5. What year is it?
6. What building is this?
7. What floor are we on?
8. What town are we in?
9. What county are we in?
10. What country are we in?

Any big change or decrease in ability to answer should alert providers and caregivers to a possibility of delirium that warrants further work-up.

Intervention: Utilizing clocks, displaying visible calendars or dates for patients, having boards that show the names of daily providers, reminding patients about upcoming tests or procedures, engaging in discussions about current events, or playing mentally stimulating games can be beneficial for delirium assessment and as therapeutic interventions.

SEE FAMILIAR FACES

Encourage daytime visits from friends and family, and limit large gatherings at night to allow the patient adequate time to rest. If family can't be present, have familiar caregivers or request hospital sitters to provide companionship and safety for patients.

OPTIMIZE CIRCADIAN RHYTHMS

Earlier in my training, it seemed more common for providers to prescribe sleep medications as a routine evening treatment. However, nowadays, nondrug approaches are increasingly favored as a first-line treatment. Melatonin may be a safer alternative to traditional medications for reducing postoperative delirium. In one study involving patients undergoing cardiothoracic, orthopedic, or liver surgeries, those who received melatonin from the night before surgery up to nine days after were found to have a 37% lower chance of developing postoperative delirium,[11] highlighting its potential as a preventative treatment in older adults. Other nonpharmacologic interventions for a bedtime routine may include a warm drink (such as herbal tea), relaxation music, guided imagery, or calming essential oils if allowed.

OPTIMIZE NUTRITION AND HYDRATION

Having family available at mealtimes can be very helpful for engaging and motivating patients to meet their caloric needs. Asking the nurse or doctor whether a patient has fluid or dietary restrictions is important for avoiding the risk of worsening a health condition. In some situations, and if approved by the physician, families may be allowed to provide food that's more appealing to the patient.

ADDRESS SENSORY IMPAIRMENT

Alerting hospital staff and healthcare providers about sensory impairments, whether it's for yourself or a loved one, is a crucial step in enhancing communication and can significantly lower the risk of delirium. Start by introducing yourself to the hospital staff and letting them know your relationship to the patient. Help your loved one navigate their surroundings, pointing out key areas like the bathroom, hallway door, phone, and call button. Prioritize clear communications by ensuring the hospital provides appropriate communication aids such as braille, large-print materials, smartphones, magnifying glasses, or interpreters as needed. Some facilities may offer preloaded communication tools and even Internet access for these tools.

BALANCE MEDICATIONS FOR PAIN AND COMFORT

This is a tricky topic because both the under- and overtreatment of pain with opioids (morphine, hydromorphone, and fentanyl) and sedatives like benzodiazepines (Ativan, Valium, and Xanax) can create delirium and lots of other complications. Nonopioid medications can always be requested and tried first or preemptively before a procedure if possible. NSAIDS and Tylenol, gabapentin, topical creams, and patches may all be options. There was a time when I was performing acupuncture in the hospital for pain control. However, those services will likely be limited and available only in certain hospitals.

STAY HYDRATED

Dehydration is an extremely common issue among elderly people, especially when they're in the hospital. Older adults are more likely to get dehydrated because their bodies change as they age. They can feel less thirsty and have kidneys that don't work as well. This risk is even higher for those with mental illness or a history of stroke. Studies have clearly shown that something as basic as hydration status can lead to confusion, delirium, constipation, urinary tract infections, fatigue, falling, and a longer stay in the hospital.[12]

BE AWARE OF CONSTIPATION

Many elderly patients suffer from constipation and difficulty with regular bowel movements when they're in the hospital. This can really affect their quality of life and make their hospital stays longer. A study looking at patients in an internal medicine ward found that 68% had constipation during their hospital stay, leading to delirium in 11% and urinary retention in 5%. Alarmingly, this study also found that constipation often goes underrecognized, with 30% of cases not receiving treatment.[13] This underscores the importance for patients, caregivers, and hospital staff to be proactive regarding its assessment and treatment.

AVOID IMMOBILITY

Whether patients are bedbound, in a wheelchair, or immobile because of a fracture or weakness from the illness that brought them to the hospital, lack of mobility is an issue to be taken seriously. Immobility is associated with the development of a series of complications that include delirium and other life-threatening conditions, such as blood clots, pneumonia, and urinary tract infections. Generalized muscle weakness and deconditioning are other major concerns of prolonged immobility. In a patient with critical illness, the loss of nearly 2% of skeletal muscle per day can be seen within the first week.[14] The longer and more severe the illness and hospitalization, the greater the chance of significant morbidity and mortality, which will impact the patient even after discharge.

These serious complications are why most hospital-trained physicians emphasize the importance of early mobilization. Physical therapy consultations need to be implemented early in a hospital stay to prevent weakness, deconditioning, and prolonged hospitalization. But aside from getting movement and exercise to avoid deconditioning, skin sores, and leg clots, another key element of these formal evaluations is to continue regular assessments of the patient's mobility status and anticipate what level of care they'll need at discharge.

Family members can ask doctors to request these consultations. They can also ask the physical therapist what level of care their loved one will likely require. Having early conversations on this topic will allow a more active partnership and conversation between the family and the providers so they can recommend realistic options.

HOSPITAL-ACQUIRED INFECTIONS

Hospital-acquired infections, also known as healthcare-associated infections (HAIs), are among the leading causes of preventable deaths among hospitalized patients.[15] These are infections that aren't present at the time of admission, are acquired after hospitalization, and can become apparent as soon as forty-eight hours after admission. This can happen in a hospital, a nursing home, surgical centers, dialysis centers, or really any other healthcare facility. Some typical HAIs include bloodstream infections, urinary tract infections from catheters, pneumonia from ventilators (or breathing machines), *Clostridium difficile* infections, and surgical site infections.

Certain patients will be at higher risk, including the very young, the very old, those with weakened immune systems due to diseases such as cancer or diabetes, and those on immune-suppressing medications (such as chemotherapy, steroids, or transplant medications). As a patient's stay in the hospital is prolonged, there's a higher chance they'll have procedures, catheters, and antibiotics, all of which can expose them to these dangerous infections. Unfortunately, the danger is more than the infection itself. Many of the organisms responsible (bacteria, viruses, and fungi) may be of the multidrug-resistant variety for which good treatments are limited, making the condition so serious and deadly.

METHICILLIN-RESISTANT *STAPHYLOCOCCUS AUREUS* (MRSA) INFECTION

You might have heard about someone in the hospital having a challenging infection caused by methicillin-resistant *Staphylococcus aureus* (MRSA). *Staphylococcus aureus* is a common bacteria found on the skin or in the nose. Research indicates that approximately a third of people have it in their nose, often without getting sick. About 2 out of every 100 people carry the more drug-resistant version, MRSA.[16] While many people carry MRSA in their noses without getting seriously ill, it causes a greater risk to immunocompromised patients or those who have undergone invasive procedures, like the use of catheters and ventilators. In these patients, MRSA can result in bloodstream infections, pneumonia, surgical site infections, sepsis, and even death.

MRSA spreads in healthcare settings when people touch infected wounds or come into contact with contaminated hands, usually those of healthcare workers. People can also carry these bacteria without being ill themselves and still pass them on to others.

CLOSTRIDIUM DIFFICILE (C. DIFF) INFECTION

Another very challenging infection we worry about in the hospital, and one my dad battled on multiple occasions, was *Clostridium difficile* (*C. diff*). This kind of bacteria causes almost a half million infections in the US and varies in symptoms, from mild, watery stools to life-threatening diarrhea and inflammation of the colon. Seniors who are receiving medical treatment, have weakened immune systems, or have spent extended periods in hospitals or nursing homes are at greatest risk. Typically, this infection can develop within days to months of starting a course of antibiotics, which, in the process of killing bad bacteria, can also remove the good bacteria that defend against *C. diff*. The CDC reports that 1 out of 6 patients can get recurrent and repeated infections in 2 to 8 weeks and that 1 in 11 people over 65 who get infected with healthcare-associated *C. diff* actually die within a month of infection.[17] They can present with varying degrees of abdominal pain, dehydration, loss of appetite, weight loss, and failure to respond to typical treatments.

Ultimately, sometimes only a fecal transplant (a procedure in which stool from a healthy donor is given to these patients) can resolve this challenging infection. So, patients should avoid unnecessary antibiotic use and let their provider know if they develop diarrhea. Prevention is key, and while families and caregivers have limited control once a loved one is hospitalized, there are some precautions that can be taken.

Of course, this is a short list out of many possible organisms and infection types that can be associated with HAIs. As stated in Chapter 1, you can review and compare data on hospital-acquired infections for different facilities you're considering. While medical staff and physicians in hospitals and healthcare facilities are very aware of necessary precautions to prevent infections, you can also play a proactive role in ensuring your safety. Here are some simple steps to protect yourself and your family from harmful germs while hospitalized:

1. **Hand Hygiene:** Ensure that every health professional interacting with you or your loved one washes their hands or uses hand sanitizer before any contact. Feel free to kindly remind them if needed.
2. **Wise Antibiotic Use:** Take antibiotics only when the doctor feels it's absolutely necessary. Taking

antibiotics unnecessarily can expose you to risks and future infections.

3. **New Infections:** Watch for signs of a new infection, such as fever, increased pain, redness, and swelling. Alert the medical team if needed.

4. **Infection Prevention:** Understand that in certain situations, healthcare providers may take extra precautions, such as using gowns and gloves, to prevent the spread of antibiotic-resistant germs. Don't hesitate to ask questions about prevention measures and express any concerns.

5. ***C. difficile* Risk:** If you've been taking antibiotics and experience severe diarrhea, let your doctor know right away.

6. **Environmental Cleanliness:** Pay attention to and express any concerns about the cleanliness of the patient's surroundings. If something doesn't seem clean, report it to the staff.

7. **Visitor Policies:** Familiarize yourself with the hospital's visitor policies, especially during infectious outbreaks.

8. **Education:** Stay informed about the patient's condition and any specific precautions required. Ask for educational materials or resources if necessary.

9. **Advocacy:** Don't hesitate to speak up if you believe additional precautions or actions are necessary.

By actively engaging in care and being vigilant about preventing infection, patients and caregivers can contribute to a safer healthcare environment and reduce the risk of hospital-acquired infections.

Hospital staff, patients, and family members all need to be aware of the serious risk a prolonged hospitalization carries and do everything they can to enable a prompt, timely, and safe discharge. For patients under the care of an experienced hospitalist, there will be proactive measures to ensure timely discharge from the first day of admission. While it may seem premature to start planning for discharge when the patient is admitted, you can never be too prepared. I suggest that you check in regularly with the hospital doctors at the time of admission and every few days after to get estimates on days until discharge.

You can also ask the doctors whether they foresee the patient being able to go home or if there may be a need for a higher level of care at a nursing home or rehab facility. In some cases, such as with a serious stroke or broken bones, it will likely be very clear in the first few days of hospitalization that a higher level of care will be needed, as the patient is unlikely to be independent at the time of discharge. Family members and caregivers can use this valuable time to start looking for help at home or even evaluate local nursing homes. While the doctors will be a great resource regarding what level of care may be required at the time of discharge, the discharge planning team, or case managers, can identify potential agencies or nursing homes that a patient's insurance covers.

The hospital team can also provide important information on what services and equipment may be needed at the time of discharge, especially if the patient is likely to go home. Your insurance company may require documentation for bedside commodes (or toilets), air mattresses, hospital beds, walkers, and even physical therapy or home safety checks. The insurance company may request doctors' notes that show why requested equipment or services are medically necessary.

Once again, the sooner these topics are thought about and discussed with the medical team, the higher the chance of an efficient discharge process. In many situations, and depending on the diagnosis, a safe discharge home may simply not be an option. This brings about the topic of potential placement options after hospitalization. In the next chapter, we'll look a little more closely at the possibilities.

TEACHABLE POINTS

1. **Risks of Prolonged Hospitalization:** Longer hospital stays increase the likelihood of adverse events and complications, including healthcare-associated infections, delirium, physical and cognitive decline (especially in the elderly), falls, and more.

2. **Reasons for Prolonged Hospitalization:** These include complex illnesses, lack of safe discharge options, family reluctance, limited nursing home availability, and insurance issues. Over half of patients with extended stays face difficulties in finding safe discharge destinations.

3. **Risk for Elderly:** Prolonged hospitalization can significantly impact older individuals, who make up a substantial portion of hospitalized patients. This highlights the need to prioritize this vulnerable group's well-being.

4. **Delirium Risk:** Altered mental abilities are common in hospitalized patients, especially the elderly. It can lead to falls, medication risks, and prolonged hospitalization. Delirium can also indicate underlying life-threatening conditions and is associated with higher mortality rates.

5. **Minimizing Delirium:** Strategies to minimize delirium include orientation assessments using calendars and boards, having familiar faces around, optimizing circadian rhythms, ensuring proper nutrition and

hydration, addressing sensory impairments, and balancing medications for pain and comfort.

6. **Hospital-Acquired Infections:** These infections, also known as healthcare-associated infections, are some of the leading causes of preventable deaths among hospitalized patients. Certain groups, like the elderly and those with weakened immune systems, are at higher risk. Prolonged hospitalization, ICU stays, and procedures increase the risk.

7. **Infection Prevention:** Practicing hand hygiene, maintaining clean surroundings, understanding visitor policies, monitoring symptoms, and advocating for infection prevention are some strategies to prevent infections while hospitalized.

Chapter 7

READY FOR DISCHARGE

At this point, you or your loved ones have avoided some major complications at the hospital and will soon be developing a discharge plan. Since we discussed the importance of thinking about discharge planning soon after hospitalization, hopefully, you're prepared to explore the options.

RETURNING HOME

While most patients can transition home without a lot of supplies, a patient may have new needs that require equipment at home. In all likelihood, the healthcare team—physical therapists, occupational therapists, nurses, and physicians—have assessed these needs before discharge. Common equipment may include home oxygen, hospital beds, mobility devices (e.g., canes, walkers, wheelchairs), bedside commodes, air mattresses, nebulizers, and more. If new medications, antibiotics, injections, urinary catheters, or wound care supplies are needed, the hospital nursing staff will provide instructions for at-home care.

At discharge, a home nursing visit order may also be initiated to monitor the patient's condition, ensure proper medication compliance, administer intravenous medication, and provide urinary catheter or wound care. If ongoing physical therapy and occupational therapy are required, a home health agency referral will be arranged.

Before discharge, it's common to have to decide whether a patient with mobility limitations should continue with physical therapy. The physical therapist typically suggests where to continue physical therapy—whether at home, in an acute rehabilitation facility, or in a nursing home—based on the patient's physical condition, mobility, strength, and ability to participate in therapy effectively. Of course, family preferences and resources impact this decision as well, including factors like insurance limitations and the availability of family support. For instance, individuals with strong family support or involved caregivers often fare well at home. On the other hand, families with limited support may find that a nursing home with round-the-clock care is the safest choice.

When Miriam, my relative, was discharged home after knee surgery, I was unimpressed with her very limited and ineffective home physical therapy program. At times, she would refuse to cooperate because she was tired or just not in the mood. I got the impression that one specific physical therapist was quick to abandon therapy as soon as Miriam resisted in the least bit. Ultimately, after a few unsatisfactory visits, we requested a different home agency and were happy with the result. The point is, if things don't work out with your first pick, contact your provider for referrals to other home health agencies for a more satisfactory outcome.

In general, I feel that home-based physical therapy often falls short of providing the aggressive and proactive exercise therapy some individuals require. If a patient can be transported to an outpatient physical therapy facility, that's typically a significantly better choice. Outpatient facilities are better equipped, offering a wider range of equipment, additional resources, and a team of therapists to more comprehensively meet the patient's needs.

If home-based physical therapy is deemed unsuitable or unsafe for a patient, a nursing home or a similar facility may be recommended. In such cases, the case manager or discharge planner will assess the doctor's and physical therapist's recommendations, along with the patient's insurance coverage, to compile a list of potential facilities for discharge. Subsequently, they'll need to coordinate with the chosen facility to determine the availability of beds on the expected discharge date.

Extensivist Programs: Bridging Inpatient-Outpatient Care

Another aspect of discharge planning that deserves special attention, especially for those with complex medical needs, is a referral to an extensivist program, which in many centers originated as the solution to helping complex patients with frequent hospital admissions—such as those with heart failure, chronic kidney disease, advanced lung disease, cancer, diabetes, or organ transplantation—transition from the hospital to the outpatient setting. An extensivist doctor, who's often a hospitalist, may get involved in a patient's care during a hospital stay or care for them soon (typically within a few days) after discharge in the outpatient setting. A referral to an extensivist program may be suggested at the time of discharge.

The program's main goals are maintaining prompt care, continuity, and safety to prevent readmissions. Extensivists often prioritize communications with a patient's primary care team and specialists, collaborating on safe discharge planning to make sure the transition back to the patient's primary care doctor is as smooth as possible. This type of specialist is typically part of a bigger extensivist program, which includes a larger team of experienced nurses, pharmacists, care coordinators, and social workers who are all experienced in caring for complex patients with frequent hospital admissions.

In my dad's case, we had the good fortune of having an extensivist who also practiced as a PCP. The comprehensive care that followed Dad in and out of the hospital was a lifesaver because it provided the continuity we needed between his many hospital admissions. Even during hospitalizations, when the extensivist wasn't available to provide direct care in the hospital, he was always very involved, communicating our family's wishes and requests to the doctors who were in charge in the hospital. If there was any confusion or clarification needed on medical history or goals of care, he easily communicated our wishes to the hospital staff. Importantly, the team made the hospital-to-home transition seamless and made sure prompt follow-up occurred within a few days after discharge.

Following a hospital discharge, the extensivist program continued to follow Dad's care closely. Regular check-ins with their dedicated pharmacist prevented medication errors. The team of nurses, *care coordinators, and social workers also provided invaluable support, which included arranging transportation to his clinic appointments, closer monitoring of labs and clinical status, and coordinating prompt care when needed to avoid a readmission. New symptoms or changes from his baseline health were addressed with the utmost urgency.*

This proactive approach led to rapid actions, such as ordering blood work or administering intravenous fluids or antibiotics, which often eliminated the need for ER visits. If you or your loved one has been admitted to a hospital more than twice in the past year, I highly advise that you ask your primary care doctors or the hospital if they have an extensivist program.

SKILLED NURSING FACILITIES AND NURSING HOMES

Most commonly, if there's what is called a "skilled need," the doctor will suggest a skilled nursing facility (SNF). A skilled need refers to therapy or treatment that can be provided only in a facility where registered nurses or physical, speech, and occupational therapists can supervise it. Qualifying needs may include wound care, intravenous therapies (antibiotics, medications, or fluids), catheter care, physical therapy, etc. Medicare, Medicaid, or private health insurance require doctors' orders for skilled nursing provided in a facility for any length of time. SNFs may also be an option for some hospice patients who can't be taken care of by family at home.

You might be curious about the distinction between a nursing home and a skilled nursing facility. While the terms *skilled nursing facility* (SNF) and *nursing home* are often used interchangeably, they mean very different levels of patient care. While both can be options for patients leaving the hospital, SNFs are much more common referrals due to their capability to provide intensive medical care and rehabilitation services. The term *nursing home* broadly covers various residential care settings, potentially including SNFs, but mainly refers to those providing long-term custodial care. The essential differences between these facilities lie in the level of medical care they offer and the professional qualifications of their staff. It's important to recognize that regulations and definitions for these care settings can differ significantly from one region to another. Generally speaking, here are some important differences:

	Skilled Nursing Facility	Nursing Home
Level of Care	SNFs offer a higher level of medical care and rehabilitation services. They're designed for individuals who require short-term medical care and rehabilitation after a hospital stay, surgery ,or illness .SNFs provide physical therapy, occupational therapy ,and speech therapy in addition to custodial care.	Nursing homes primarily provide custodial care, which includes assistance with activities of daily living (ADLs), such as bathing, dressing, eating, and mobility.
Medical Services	SNFs have a higher ratio of medical staff to residents and are equipped to provide more intensive medical care .They often have physicians ,therapists, and other healthcare professionals on-site to manage complex medical conditions.	While nursing homes have medical staff ,such as nurses and nurse practitioners ,they may not have the same level of specialized medical care available in an SNF.

	Skilled Nursing Facility	Nursing Home
Length of Stay	SNF stays are usually short-term ,ranging from a few days to a few months. They provide specialized care and rehabilitation until the individual is well enough to return home or transition to another care setting.	Residents in nursing homes typically stay for an extended period ,often long term or indefinitely, especially if they have chronic conditions that require ongoing care.
Payment and Insurance	Medicare often covers SNF care for qualified individuals ,especially if they've had a recent hospital stay and require skilled nursing and therapy services .Medicaid may also cover SNF care for eligible individuals.	Nursing home care is often privately paid for by individuals or their families ,although long-term care insurance or Medicaid may cover some costs for eligible individuals.

NURSE-TO-PATIENT RATIO

It's important to note that, although these facilities have 24-hour staffing, the level of care is significantly lower than in hospitals. While federal laws have provided some general guidelines for optimal ratios, there's great variability between the states and local facilities on how staffing ratios are enforced. For example, California law requires all nursing homes to provide at least 3.2 nursing hours per resident day (HPRD). That means a resident gets a little over 3 hours of interaction from a *combination* of licensed nurses and certified nursing assistants (CNA). The number of patients a single nurse may oversee can vary widely; typically, a nurse may care for 20 patients during the day shift, but this number can increase to 30 patients during the night shift, when resident activity is lower and less frequent monitoring is required. It is known that a majority of those regulated hours per resident day (HPRD) are actually delivered by a certified nursing assistant (CNA) rather than a registered nurse.[1]

Recall from Chapter 2 that a certified nursing assistant (CNA) provides basic healthcare, like taking blood pressure, assisting with eating, and bathing. They typically undergo only a few months of training after high school. That means a nursing home patient receives a small fraction of care from a fully trained nurse in an entire day. You can imagine how frightening this can be for someone who has a lot of needs or requires close monitoring. There are several studies showing that employing a greater number of RNs is associated with reduced pressure ulcers, infections, pain, weight loss, dehydration, antipsychotic use, and mortality rates.[2]

Unfortunately, a significant number of nursing homes aren't meeting the required staffing levels to ensure safety. Nearly 60% of facilities have been found to have total nurse staffing levels below what is expected based on the needs of their residents. And a quarter of these facilities are operating with staffing levels that are critically low.[3]

While there are federal government proposals suggesting nurse-to-patient staffing ratios, these proposals can't dictate state-specific policies. Each state is responsible for establishing and enforcing its own staffing ratios. In states with formal laws, there are mechanisms for obtaining exemptions and various challenges related to reporting. In the absence of formal laws, healthcare facilities may rely on their own policies to determine nurse-to-patient ratios. In other words, the enforcement of rules and regulations concerning these ratios in nursing homes can be somewhat unclear and variable.

During my research, I ran across one resource that allows users to search for specific nursing homes and access data regarding the number of patients being cared for by registered nurses. Doing a search for Los Angeles nursing homes, I noticed a significant variation in the number of residents attended to by nurses on their best and worst staffed days. This range could vary widely, from 5 to 130 residents receiving care from a single nurse. While it would be challenging to track these numbers from facility to facility, it may be a factor to consider when visiting and getting information from a list of different facilities.

PERSONAL INSIGHT: MIRIAM'S NURSING HOME PLACEMENT

In my family's personal experience, the nurse-to-patient ratios became much more than an abstract concept. When my relative, Miriam, ultimately needed nursing home placement, we were shocked to learn that the actual nurse-to-patient ratio at her facility was 35 patients to a single nurse.

But even more surprising than that was the frequency of physician visits and evaluations. Shortly after her admission, we were informed that a physician evaluation and exam were most likely going to happen within 72 hours of admission to the nursing facility. Thereafter, physician visits were only required once every 30 days for the first 90 days after admission and at least once every 60 days thereafter.

When it comes to your loved ones, please inquire about these very important topics so you know what to expect. Miriam's experience opened our eyes to the importance of being informed and proactive when it comes to the care of family members in nursing facilities.

QUESTIONS TO ASK WHEN EVALUATING NURSING HOME FACILITIES

When hospital staff or discharge planners provide you with a list of nursing home options, consider visiting the different facilities if time allows. During your visits, direct these essential questions to the nursing facility administrators. This information can be incredibly helpful when making your decision about choosing a nursing home.

1. Nursing Staffing and Care
— What is the nurse-to-patient ratio during the day and night shifts?
— How many staff members are available per shift, and what are their qualifications?
— Are there licensed nurses available around the clock?

2. Physician and Medical Care
— How often do physicians visit the facility to see residents?
— Are physicians available for emergencies?
— Are there specific physicians assigned to the facility?
— Which hospitals are the facility's physicians affiliated with in case of hospitalization or emergencies?
— How are medications managed, and is there a pharmacist on staff?
— How are medical records kept, and can family members access them?

3. Room and Accommodations
— What types of rooms are available (e.g., private, semiprivate)?

— How are room assignments made?

— Is there a waiting list for specific room types?

4. Services and Activities

— What medical services and therapies are provided on-site?

— Are there recreational and social activities for residents?

— How often are activities and outings organized?

5. Dining and Nutrition

— Can residents choose their meals, and are special dietary needs accommodated?

— Are family members allowed to join residents for meals or bring food from home?

6. Safety and Security

— What safety measures are in place to prevent falls and accidents?

— How does the facility handle emergencies and evacuations?

7. Communication with Family

— How does the facility communicate with family members about a resident's condition?

— What is the process for resolving concerns or complaints?

8. Financial Concerns and Insurance

— What are the costs, and how is billing handled?

— Does the facility accept Medicare, Medicaid, or other insurance?

— Are there additional fees or charges for specific services?

9. Quality of Life
— How does the facility promote resident engagement and independence?
— Can you observe a typical day at the facility?

The answers to these questions should help provide a better understanding of the nursing home you're considering. Additionally, it's essential to trust your instincts and consider the overall atmosphere and interactions you observe during your visit.

OTHER TYPES OF FACILITIES

LONG-TERM ACUTE-CARE HOSPITAL (LTACH)

LTACHs provide the highest level of care outside of a typical acute-care hospital and are intended for patients who have experienced prolonged hospitalizations or extended stays in the ICU. These facilities provide care for those requiring complex medical management, such as prolonged use of or weaning off the ventilator (breathing machine), complex wound or burn care, ongoing dialysis or kidney failure, and multiple intravenous therapies. In this setting, patients are followed closely by a physician daily, and there's access to specialists as needed.

While these facilities can deliver a very high level of care for severely ill patients, it's important to realize that needing such placement in itself suggests the possibility of a poor long-term prognosis. This is highlighted by a study among Medicare patients requiring LTACH-level care, which calculated that patients' average survival time after being transferred was about 8.3 months. Following this type of care, nearly half never achieved a 60-day recovery, a third passed away, and many spent their remaining days as inpatients.[4]

ACUTE REHABILITATION

These are short-term placement facilities and may be licensed as inpatient hospitals or rehab units within a hospital. They provide much closer medical supervision for those with higher levels of functioning who have the desire and ability to participate in physical therapy and occupational therapy for three hours a day, five times a week. The aim is to provide more intensive physical and occupational therapies and have patients return home. Physicians evaluate patients several times a week or even on a daily basis if needed. Some typical medical conditions requiring such care include stroke, brain and spine injury, fractures, or joint replacement. In general, if a patient meets the criteria for this high level of intensive care, it's typically better for them to be admitted to a facility offering this level of care instead of a nursing home.

In a study looking at the sickest stroke survivors, discharge to a skilled nursing facility (SNF) had a striking mortality rate of 64%, whereas those transferred to an acute rehabilitation facility experienced a significantly lower mortality rate of 29.6% at one year. The study highlights that for the sickest patients, who may still have the potential for recovery, admission to these types of facilities with intensive therapy and medical supervision can significantly impact their long-term outcomes.[5]

CHOOSING THE RIGHT FACILITY

To put things in perspective, it's important to note that the level of monitoring and care differs significantly among all these types of facilities. Therefore, when considering discharge options, be aware of the limitations and realities regarding posthospital care.

TEACHABLE POINTS

1. **Home Transition:** Consider equipment needs and care instructions when transitioning home from the hospital.

2. **Physical Therapy Choices:** The decision about where to continue physical therapy depends on the physician's and physical therapist's recommendations, as well as the patient's condition, preferences, insurance coverage, and family support.

3. **Nursing Home versus Skilled Nursing Facility (SNF):** Understand the distinction between nursing homes and skilled nursing facilities (SNFs). SNFs offer higher medical care and rehabilitation services for short-term stays, while nursing homes focus on custodial care for long-term residents.

4. **Nurse-to-Patient Ratios:** Be aware that staffing ratios vary among facilities. Hospitals provide more intensive care, while nursing homes may have lower staffing levels, impacting patient safety.

5. **Nursing Home Staffing:** Higher RN staffing levels lead to better outcomes, including lower mortality rates and reduced complications. Pay attention to nursing staff qualifications when choosing a facility.

6. **State-Specific Staffing Regulations:** Staffing ratios are determined by state regulations, impacting the quality of care. Enforcement varies, with some states having formal laws and others relying on facility policies.

7. **Nursing Home Visits:** When visiting nursing home facilities, ask essential questions about staffing, medical care, accommodations, services, dining, safety, communication, and quality of life. Trust your observations and instincts during the visit.

8. **Long-Term Acute-Care Hospitals (LTACHs):** LTACHs provide ICU-level care outside acute hospitals but often indicate a poor long-term prognosis.

9. **Acute Rehabilitation:** Acute rehabilitation facilities offer intensive physical therapy for patients before returning home. They provide closer medical supervision and are a better option for high-functioning patients with specific conditions, like stroke survivors.

CHAPTER 8

INTENSIVE CARE UNIT AND END OF LIFE

Some patients may require intensive care during their hospitalization but lack the knowledge and awareness of the risks and consequences associated with such care. Patients might be too ill or confused to realize they've been transferred to the ICU, and there may be insufficient time to inform families in advance. While the goal is to save lives through aggressive interventions, it's crucial that patients and families fully understand the procedures involved. What's considered necessary for a younger patient with a sudden cardiac arrest may not be appropriate for an elderly patient with advanced cancer or multiple-organ failure.

In the last few years, our family experienced multiple friends and family members who required such high-level care and hospitalization.

When Miriam was hospitalized, we didn't know that in a span of 24 hours, the hospital would call a half dozen times in the middle of the night to ask if we wanted her transferred to the ICU. It was the same situation with my dad when he was hospitalized for the last time. Both he and Miriam were over 80 and had serious health conditions—

Miriam with dementia and Parkinson's disease, and Dad with advanced heart, kidney, and liver failure. Neither one of them had expressed their wishes for end-of-life care or selected a health agent.

So, imagine getting a call at 2:00 a.m. and being shocked out of sleep to be asked over and over, "Are you sure you want her transferred to the ICU?" "Are you sure you want to prolong her suffering?" "Are you sure you want to put a big, painful tube through her nose that will travel to her stomach to give her medications and to treat her life-threatening high potassium?" "Are you sure you want to put a big, painful catheter in her neck to deliver medication because her current blood pressure is dangerously low, and she might not survive the night?"

Despite knowing all the discomfort and pain associated with the nasogastric tube, invasive intravenous lines, and urinary catheters, it's still hard to refuse many of those interventions when you're faced with potentially losing a loved one. In my opinion, the way we physicians expect patients and families to answer questions in a time of crisis is really not the best approach. Being on the receiving end of such frantic calls from hospital doctors, I witnessed the use of too many medical words and concepts that were too technical and complex for the average nonmedical person. Frequently, there's a pressing need for answers to questions that can be challenging even for physicians, much less the average family member.

In this chapter, I'll delve a bit deeper into some of the reasons someone might need the ICU and how you can make that decision with great consideration and care. I'll also cover some therapies provided in the ICU in case you receive an unexpected, urgent call from a doctor. It can be somewhat less stressful if you have some understanding of what to anticipate in such a situation.

WHY SOMEONE MAY NEED THE ICU

An adult patient may be transferred or admitted to the ICU for life-threatening conditions that require a higher level of attention and care, such as:

1. Respiratory Failure: This is defined as an inability to breathe independently to bring sufficient oxygen to the body, brain, and organs. Severe respiratory failure to the point of needing a ventilator or a machine is presumed to impact 20% to 40% patients in an ICU.[1] There are many reasons for respiratory or lung failure, but some common causes include lung infection (pneumonia), asthma, brain injury, cardiac arrest, drug overdose, overwhelming sepsis, or an infection in the bloodstream. Another life-threatening cause of respiratory failure is acute respiratory distress syndrome (ARDS). It's thought that nearly a quarter of mechanically ventilated patients in an ICU meet criteria for this condition. It's a type of lung injury that can occur in critically ill patients, causing fluid to collect in the lungs. Looking at one study, we see that mortality from ARDS ranges from 35% to 46% based on its severity.[2]

2. Lower Level of Consciousness: If a patient is unresponsive after a severe brain injury, intoxication, trauma, or stroke, they may require close monitoring of vitals and labs in the ICU. Those who are altered, can't protect their airways, or have weakened abilities to breathe and get sufficient oxygen may also require ventilators.

3. Shock: The disruption or inadequate flow of blood and oxygen to the brain, lungs, heart, or kidneys occurs when blood pressure falls or is too weak to support the body's proper function. It may occur from a weakened heart (heart failure), heart attack, irregular heart rhythm, bleeding, severe infection, or extreme fluid loss, to name a few causes. Treatment depends on the reasons for the shock, but the goal is improving blood pressure and blood flow to the organs. This may be accomplished by transfusions, fluids, antibiotics, or medications that can improve the heart's ability to pump blood throughout the body.

4. Postsurgery Needs: Some patients are routinely transferred to the ICU for a short time after certain types of surgery for closer monitoring. They may be generally healthy people with a scheduled surgery that's more complex and requires greater nursing care, such as major vascular or cardiac surgery. In other instances, some patients require ICU admission due to serious complications after surgery, such as unexpected irregular heart rhythms, difficulty breathing, or excessive bleeding.

PROCEDURES AND THERAPIES

CPR (CARDIOPULMONARY RESUSCITATION)

This is an emergency lifesaving procedure commonly done when someone's breathing or heartbeat has stopped. It combines chest compressions with rescue breaths, which can be administered mouth-to-mouth or using a bag-mask device in a hospital setting to deliver oxygen. The primary goal of CPR is to maintain blood circulation and ensure a supply of oxygen to vital organs.

If CPR is delivered promptly in the first few minutes of cardiac arrest, it can double or triple a person's chance of survival.[3] In the context of in-hospital cardiac arrest and CPR, a person's likelihood of being discharged from the hospital is influenced by various factors, including age and heart rhythm. In 2017, the reported hospital discharge rate was approximately around 25%.[4]

While CPR can save a life, it's essential to also discuss the risks, which may be noteworthy—especially if the patient is already very ill, is elderly, or has poor baseline functioning. The most common complications from CPR are brain injury and cognitive changes (up to 50%),[5] rib (up to 30%) and sternum (up to 20%) fractures,[6] vomiting and aspiration, and risk of damage to other organs.

Complications, such as broken bones and ribs, are more common in the elderly due to their thinning bones and loss of muscle mass. This happened to Dad when he had a cardiac arrest during his last week of hospitalization before passing away. It was easy to see how his frail and thin body wouldn't tolerate the pounding on his chest, which gave him extensive bruises and painful broken bones. While he somehow miraculously survived the CPR and lack of heart activity for slightly longer than 10 minutes, he survived only two more days before we were urged to stop all care.

Looking back, I wish Dad had a better understanding of CPR and its consequences. While some may find the risks of CPR acceptable, it's crucial to understand that approximately half the time, CPR leads to the need for intubation[7]—a procedure that requires connection to a breathing machine. This significantly complicates the situation. Studies indicate that certain patients—such as frail nursing home patients, those with dementia, and patients with terminal cancer—have very low survival rates (around 0% to 5%) after CPR.[8] So, in some subsets of patients, we should consider the risks and benefits of not only CPR but also the subsequent high risk of getting intubated.

INTUBATION

While oxygen can be delivered via different devices—such as a nasal cannula (prongs to the nose), face mask, or high-flow nasal cannula on a regular medical floor—there is a limit to the amount that can be delivered in such a manner. If these simpler and less invasive systems can't safely and sufficiently oxygenate the body, a more invasive tube is inserted into the mouth and trachea (windpipe). This tube connects to a ventilator that does the job of breathing and delivers oxygen to the body. A ventilator is a life support machine. As discussed above, respiratory failure from various causes (loss of consciousness, extreme sleepiness, and cardiac arrest) often leads to intubation. A large portion of patients who receive CPR also require intubation for optimal airway management.

Intubation poses a higher risk of complications in patients who are obese, have facial trauma, have agitation, or are in urgent situations. Potential issues include injuries to the mouth, throat, or trachea, and more severe problems like aspiration, lung infections, and cardiovascular changes. This risk increases with age; for instance, intubation of older adults (65+) in the emergency department carries a 33% in-hospital mortality rate, rising to 50% for those aged 90+. Survivors often face prolonged ventilation, severe disability, and reduced quality of life.[9]

SERIOUS COMPLICATIONS OF INTUBATION:[10]

Complication	Incidence	Explanation
Cardiovascular Instability	42.6% of patients	Significant drop in blood pressure or need for increased support to maintain blood pressure during or after intubation.
Severe Hypoxemia	9.3% of patients	Dangerously low levels of oxygen in the blood during or immediately after intubation.
Cardiac Arrest	3.1% of patients	Heart stops beating during or immediately after intubation.
Esophageal Intubation	5.6% of patients	Tube accidentally placed in the esophagus instead of the trachea.
New Onset Cardiac Arrhythmia	5.6% of patients	Heart rhythm problems occurring during or after intubation.
Difficult Intubation	4.7% of patients	Challenges or repeated attempts needed to successfully place the intubation tube.
Aspiration of Gastric Contents	3.9% of patients	Stomach contents entering the lungs during intubation, posing risk of infection.

INTRAVENOUS ACCESS

You've likely seen small intravenous lines placed in a patient's arms or hands for administering fluids and medication. They're often required on a regular medical or surgical floor and are changed every few days. In emergencies or ICU transfers, you might be asked to consent to a more invasive procedure, where a catheter is inserted into a large vein, usually in the neck or occasionally in the groin. These lines are called central venous lines or shortened to central lines. They're necessary for delivering medications that could irritate smaller veins accessed through peripheral lines, including antibiotics, intravenous fluids, and blood products, allowing multiple infusions simultaneously.

The risks and complications are considerably higher than peripheral lines, putting the patient at risk for various immediate complications, such as puncturing the artery (4.2% to 9.3%), bleeding (4.7%), and lung collapse (1%).[11] Complications that may arise in the days or weeks following placement include clot formation and infections. In fact, patients with central lines may face a 10% to 30% risk of serious health complications or even death if a serious bloodstream infection occurs.[12] If a patient is transferred to an ICU, in all likelihood, there will be a need for a central line or similar type of access.

CENTRAL LINE COMPLICATIONS: [13]

Immediate Complication	Incidence	Explanation
Arterial Injury	Less than 1%	Injuring an artery during catheter placement. Most common in femoral (groin) catheters.
Arterial Puncture	4.2% to 9.3%	Puncturing an artery during catheter placement.
Hematoma Formation	Up to 4.7%	Forming a hematoma, a collection of blood outside blood vessels.
Pulmonary Complications (Pneumothorax, Pneumomediastinum)	Up to 1%	Lung-related issues, like air in the chest cavity, during catheter placement. More common in subclavian (near collarbone) catheters.
Nerve Injury	Up to 1.6%	Causing injury to a nerve during the procedure. Damage can occur to nerves that impact voice, arm movement, and breathing. Recovery may take up to 6 to 12 months.

The table below is a list of delayed complications that can occur weeks to months after central line placement.[14]

Delayed Complication	Incidence	Explanation
Catheter Breakage	More common with long-term subclavian catheters	The catheter can break, especially in long-term use, which can lead to serious health issues.
Blood Clots in Veins	Varies, up to 41% in cancer patients	Formation of blood clots in the vein where the catheter is placed, causing swelling and redness. Subclavian catheters (near collarbone) have lowest risk, while femoral (groin) lines have highest.
Swelling in Head and Neck (Superior Vena Cava Syndrome)	Estimated 1 in 1,000 cases	Rare condition with swelling of the head and neck due to vein blockage near the heart.
Narrowing of Veins (Venous Stenosis)	Up to 41% of cases	The vein where the catheter is placed can become narrow, sometimes needing medical intervention.
Serious Bloodstream Infections	80–189 in 100,000 patients per year	In a sample of 100,000 patients with central venous catheters, between 80 and 189 are expected to get serious infections over a year.

VASOPRESSORS

Vasopressors are a powerful class of drugs that constrict blood vessels to help patients with low blood pressure. Without good blood pressure, you aren't able to get adequate blood and oxygen to your vital organs. While intravenous fluids, like saline, may be tried initially to help with low blood pressure, a critically ill patient may need help with additional vasopressors. These medications typically require central lines. Some common drugs in this class include phenylephrine (or Neo-Synephrine), norepinephrine (or Levophed), epinephrine, dopamine, and dobutamine. They may be used in various conditions, such as with heart attacks, sepsis, major infections, extensive blood loss, shock, and heart failure, and after CPR. In fact, if blood pressure doesn't improve with fluids and one of these medications is required, it necessitates transfer to an ICU. Complications of these therapies include irregular heart rhythms, heart attacks, headache, nausea, and inadequate blood flow to the extremities, causing necrosis (death of tissue) in the tips of fingers and toes.

The use of vasopressors can indicate the severity of a patient's condition. A study on vasopressor therapy and the risk of hospital death indicated that the number and dose of vasopressors used are significant indicators of a patient's condition.[15] Patients requiring two or more vasopressors at full dose experienced a mortality rate of over 80%, which increased to over 90% for those receiving three or more vasopressors at full dose. In other words, as the intensity of vasopressor therapy increases, the chances of survival decrease. This information can help families make well-informed decisions.

I unfortunately had the experience of caring for a friend who spent an extended period in the ICU on multiple vasopressors. This was due to family disagreements over whether to continue life support or withdraw it. During this time, my friend began to develop blackened toes, fingers, and nose, which is a clear sign of gangrene and tissue death resulting from prolonged use of vasopressors. The distressing images and my dear friend's suffering during his final moments left a lasting and disturbing impact on me.

My father required the maximum dose of three vasopressors to maintain his blood pressure, with no improvement day after day. It became evident that he would never recover enough to leave the ICU. Ultimately, this realization was a significant factor in our decision to discontinue his care in the ICU and allow him to pass peacefully.

FEEDING TUBE

A nasogastric feeding tube is suggested if the patient is unable to get nutrition on their own for a prolonged period and can tolerate feeding through a tube inserted in the nose or mouth. Feeding is best started early and within 48 hours of admission to the ICU or initiation of mechanical ventilation. Studies suggest that early feeding may decrease the risk of infections and improve mortality, yet larger studies are needed.[16] Experts believe that giving food early in the treatment can help the gut stay healthy, support the immune system, improve blood flow, and decrease loss of muscle mass.[17] While it's always preferable to feed through the gastrointestinal tract rather than an intravenous catheter, it may not be safe to insert or use a feeding tube. In those cases, an intravenous feeding can support nutritional needs.

DIALYSIS

When people are very sick, their kidneys may not work well, and waste materials build up in their blood. Kidney failure is a common complication in the ICU and may lead to fluid buildup, elevated levels of potassium (which is dangerous to the heart), acid-base imbalances, and toxin buildup, which increases the risk of confusion and bleeding. Dialysis helps clean the blood and address these complications.

It's important to understand that in the ICU, kidney failure and the initiation of dialysis are frequently part of multiorgan failure and can be very serious, with a death rate ranging from 60% to 84%.[18] These rates can vary depending on the specific patient population, clinical setting, and other factors, but they indicate a significant risk associated with the need to start dialysis in the ICU. There are several types of dialysis, but for our purposes, we'll focus only on those you may encounter during an ICU stay.

Hemodialysis

During hemodialysis, a patient's blood is carefully drawn out of their body, where it's cleaned by a special machine that removes waste products and extra fluids. After this cleaning process, the cleaned blood is returned to the patient's body. This treatment typically takes around three to four hours and is usually conducted a few times a week. Hemodialysis is essential for patients who need rapid and effective cleansing of their blood, which is often the case for critically ill individuals.

Continuous Renal Replacement Therapy (CRRT)

This type of dialysis is a preferred choice for those with severe medical conditions in the intensive care setting. It's more suitable for patients who can't tolerate the rapid fluid and waste removal, may have lower blood pressures, or are on multiple vasopressors. It's a continuous and gentle blood-cleansing process that operates 24/7, ensuring a gradual and steady removal of waste and excess fluids from the body. In one study looking at 15-day survival for patients on CRRT, 84% of patients didn't survive.[19]

Having had multiple family members undergo dialysis, both in acute and chronic settings, I'm far too familiar with the risks and potential complications. Typically, these include severe drops in blood pressure, frequent infections, blood clots, and severe muscle cramps. My father, who began hemodialysis in his early eighties and continued the treatment for three years until his passing, faced every single one of these challenges on many occasions. Among them, the most debilitating were the severe episodes of low blood pressure and intensely painful muscle cramps, which persisted until his final moments. In his last week, the ICU doctors reluctantly offered CRRT, knowing his grim prognosis well.

SEDATION AND ANALGESIA

In the ICU, when people are very sick, they might feel pain or discomfort because of their illness or treatments. Doctors give a range of medicines called sedatives (which calm or induce sleep) or analgesics (which relieve pain) to help manage pain, anxiety, and agitation in critically ill patients. These medicines can make a person feel relaxed. They might be used to make someone sleepy for a medical procedure. However, these sedatives and analgesics come with potential risks. Insufficient use can result in continued discomfort, while excessive use may lead to slowed breathing, sudden drops in blood pressure, delirium, confusion (particularly in elderly patients), muscle weakness, withdrawal symptoms, and delayed awakening with grogginess. It's a delicate balance to ensure the patient's comfort without unwanted complications.

POST-INTENSIVE CARE SYNDROME (PICS)

While my father's health journey ended in the ICU, a majority of patients will receive lifesaving interventions that stabilize their health and allow them to transfer back out to the medical floor or home. However, I want to discuss a topic that was never discussed when I went through my medical training. While ICU survival has improved in recent years, it's clear that many patients don't return to their former level of physical, emotional, and psychological functioning for months or even years. This condition, called the post-intensive care syndrome (PICS), has a significant impact on a patient's quality of life and needs to be addressed both during and after hospitalization.

Symptoms of this disorder may include cognitive challenges, such as poor organization, memory loss, and difficulty with concentration. New mood disorders, such as anxiety, depression, and even post-traumatic stress disorder (PTSD), can be prominent. Physical symptoms include insomnia, trouble breathing, weakness, fatigue, and worsening mobility. Studies estimate the frequency of some of these changes as indicated below.[20]

- ICU-acquired weakness, described as occurring in nearly half the patients who are in the ICU for a week or longer and possibly requiring a year to recover.
- Cognitive changes, which impact as many as 25% to 75% of patients after an ICU stay. Prior cognitive changes, advanced age, duration of ICU delirium, alcoholism, low blood pressure, need for prolonged intubation, and need for dialysis can be some of the factors that increase risks. Some people improve within a year, and some may never go back to baseline.
- Depression, anxiety, and PTSD can impact nearly a third to half of patients in the first year after ICU discharge.[21] People younger than 65 with a history of depression and anxiety and physical dependence have increased risk.

SOME STRATEGIES THAT CAN BE HELPFUL FOR REDUCTION OF PICS INCLUDE:

- Minimizing heavy sedation and pain medications as much as possible
- Encouraging physical therapy and movement as soon as possible
- Identifying and treating depression, anxiety, and PTSD with therapies and medication as needed
- Implementing strategies for optimal sleep and nutrition
- Early recognition, evaluation, and treatment to address and minimize persistent and long-term symptoms

POST-INTENSIVE CARE SYNDROME-FAMILY (PICS-F)

Caregivers and families can also suffer from profound mental health effects, such as anxiety, depression, insomnia, and PTSD when their loved ones are hospitalized in the intensive care unit (ICU). Psychiatrists can play a key role in the diagnosis and management of PICS-F. This is particularly important to recognize, evaluate, and treat due to the rapidly growing population of both older ICU survivors and their family members.

The chart below demonstrates the high prevalence of these mental health disorders not only during a loved one's hospitalization but also for six months after.

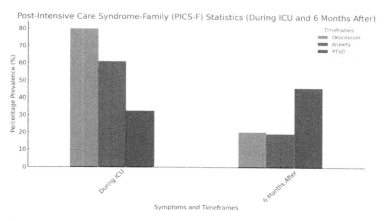

Depression, Anxiety, and PTSD Symptoms for Post-Intensive Care Syndrome-Family (PICS-F) During ICU Stays and 6 Months after ICU Discharge[22]

Family members, including parents of babies and children as well as those of adult patients, can experience negative mental health effects lasting longer than four years after intensive care, making it challenging for these family members to effectively take care of the patient once they are back home from the hospital.[23]

This highlights the important need for self-care, optimal sleep, exercise, nutrition, and support for all involved, not just the critically ill patient.

WITHDRAWAL OF CARE

Withdrawal of care in the ICU is an emotionally charged decision that means life-sustaining treatments will be stopped when it's determined they no longer serve the patient's goals or are causing too much suffering. In these cases, medical teams have frank discussions with the family to make sure that the patient's wishes are respected. The process often involves gradually reducing or discontinuing mechanical ventilation, vasopressors, and other life-support measures. The withdrawal of care isn't a decision taken lightly; it requires careful deliberation and open communication between medical teams and families to ensure that the patient's comfort, quality of life, and dignity remain the focus.

I've often seen that patients and families are quick to embrace aggressive lifesaving procedures, with the default setting frequently leaning toward full code status. However, less discussed are the grief, blame, and guilt that can accompany the withdrawal of these life-sustaining treatments. This is why it's so important for patients and families to fully understand what choosing these aggressive therapies entails, including the potential consequences and hardships that may follow. The decision to opt for lifesaving measures should be made only after careful consideration and open conversations about the patient's values, preferences, and realistic outcomes. It's crucial to acknowledge that the decision to withdraw care is, without a doubt, a heart-wrenching one. Rushed decisions in the hospital and ICU aren't ideal, as they can result in immense stress, anxiety, and discomfort for both patients and families. That's why it's crucial to prioritize advance planning and have in-depth discussions about goals of care, ideally before hospitalization.

When there's disagreement among the medical team, patients, and families, it may be necessary to consider family meetings, seek second opinions or hospital transfers, and involve the ethics committee. These steps can help families come to terms with their choices and find a sense of peace during challenging times.

COMFORT CARE AND HOSPICE

If it's determined that end-of-life care isn't imminent within hours or a day, the medical team may suggest transitioning the patient to comfort care outside the ICU. Comfort care focuses on providing relief from pain and distressing symptoms, ensuring a peaceful and dignified experience during a patient's final moments. When the patient is expected to have a few days to weeks, hospice care may be recommended. Hospice is a specialized form of care designed to provide comfort, emotional support, and symptom management in the final stages of life. Patients and families can coordinate with the case manager or discharge planner to determine whether hospice care at home or in a facility is the most suitable option.

TEACHABLE POINTS

1. **ICU Admissions:** ICU admissions often result from critical conditions, like respiratory failure, cardiac arrest, infections, strokes, trauma, and shock.

2. **Procedure Risks and Care Goals:** Learn about lifesaving ICU procedures, including intubation, vasopressors, and CPR, along with the associated risks. Consider how these interventions align with a patient's care goals and preferences, especially in high-risk patients with advanced age, dementia, or advanced cancer.

3. **Long-Term Consequences:** Consider the long-term consequences of ICU care, including weakness, fatigue, mobility decline, and cognitive impairments that can persist for months or years.

4. **Early Decision-Making:** In emergencies, emphasize the importance of making early decisions about invasive treatments and discussing them consistently with healthcare providers and family.

5. **End-of-Life Care:** Explore the delicate decisions involved in end-of-life care, discussing withdrawal of care, comfort care, and hospice. Understand the emotional aspects and the importance of patient wishes during these challenging times.

6. **Post-Intensive Care Syndrome (PICS) and (PICS-F):** Recognize the conditions affecting many ICU survivors and their families. Proactively address these issues during and after hospitalization.

CONCLUSION

Dad always spoke as if he would live forever. End-of-life wasn't a topic he would have ever liked mentioned or discussed. In his early eighties, one of his biggest concerns was the inconvenience that would come about the next time he would need to change his pacemaker battery—and that was going to be when he turned 90! He either didn't want to accept his fragile health or simply thought he could outsmart it.

During his final week, when he was admitted to an unfamiliar hospital near his home and had doctors who were strangers to him and his medical history, our challenges with the healthcare system grew. Seeing his dire physical state and near unresponsiveness, the doctors hesitated and delayed his transfer to the ICU. They brought in various specialists and spoke with me in harsh words, suggesting that I was only prolonging his suffering by escalating his care. They were guilting me for being the bad, unreasonable daughter who was oblivious to his poor prognosis. To them, he was just an elderly, frail, dying man. They had no knowledge of his remarkable history of defying death on numerous occasions. They neither knew nor cared that just 24 hours earlier, I'd been diligently visiting different nursing homes in search of the most suitable place where he could continue his physical therapy after a fall and pelvic fracture.

As a hospitalist who'd taken care of many similar patients, I was well aware of how little time he had left. The increased risk of death during the first three months after a fall and fracture was a statistic I knew well. Yet I also knew how he'd outlived so many other health scares. Despite knowing the odds against him, I prayed for yet one more miracle.

While there's no magic formula that can tell you with 100% certainty how much longer a person has, certain things are known. We know that a patient's frailty, functional status, chronic conditions, and baseline health have a lot to do with their prognosis. We know that with each passing decade—and especially after major heart attacks, strokes, kidney failure, cancer, and dementia—the additive risk accumulates, making the chances of meaningful recovery very slim. Yet there are still no easy answers, even when you're a doctor who knows all the statistics.

I'll be the first to admit that my doctor brain was thinking, *Why are these doctors even asking me if I want my dad transferred to the ICU? He's over 80 years old with practically no functioning organ left in his body. Of course, he isn't going to do well.* At the same time, my daughter brain was even angrier, wondering why the hospital staff wasn't doing more, why they were taking so long to get his medications, and why they were so resistant to giving us a little more time. And there was definitely a part of me that was frustrated and resentful that Dad hadn't made his wishes clear earlier, because then at least I wouldn't be in the painful situation of deciding for him.

Since he'd never expressed his wishes for end-of-life care and had such a dramatic change in his condition—going from doing well in rehab to being barely responsive in a matter of hours—I pleaded with the doctors to give us 48 hours to see which way things would go. Would he improve without too much intervention and be able to go to his nursing facility for physical therapy as previously planned? Would he be able to go home and live a few weeks or months longer? I didn't think a couple of days was too much to ask for.

Shortly after the hospital admission, his blood pressure started plummeting to frighteningly low levels. I cried and kissed him goodbye, thinking he might not make it through that first night. Since I'd asked to wait for an extra day or two, I agreed to his transfer to the ICU if it was needed. There he would get closer monitoring and some low-dose vasopressors, the medications that would support his blood pressure. I didn't think intubation or a ventilator would be in his best interest. I thought CPR, shock, or intravenous medication (in essence, a limited code), if needed during those 48 hours, would have fewer long-term complications and could buy us a little time. I decided that if he didn't wake up, the decision would be clear, and we would stop all support.

Things were much the same on Saturday, after his transfer to the ICU, and I kept wondering how his frail body had endured so much. He'd never been confused or unresponsive during any of his prior hospitalizations, so seeing him this way was new and frightening. Sunday rolled around, and I drove to the hospital thinking it was going to be the day that we would tell the doctors to stop all care. Tears rolled down my face just thinking about having this dreaded conversation with the doctors.

I walked into the ICU on Sunday morning and was shocked to see Dad sitting up, alert and smiling. I simply couldn't believe it. He seemed a bit tired, but his mind was clear, and he talked as if nothing had happened. I filled him in on the events of the prior two days, since he had no memory of them. In my culture, talking about death and one's wishes at the end of life is taboo, so I had to be a bit more creative. I told him that I'd thought he'd planned to leave us. He quickly responded with a big smile, saying, "I'm in no hurry to go, my dear. I'm just fine right here."

I saw this as an opportunity to ask just one more time what his wishes were. His doctors had been persistently asking me for two days why I was pushing for him to have such aggressive care when his chances of survival were so slim. I asked the nurse to call the main hospitalist so he could be present and hear it directly from my dad's mouth.

The nurse told Dad that the doctors needed to know what they should do if his heart stopped or he couldn't breathe on his own. It was a question I'd asked my patients so many times without thinking twice. I was speechless when Dad said, without hesitation, that he would want everything done. Chest compressions, shock, vasopressors, antibiotics, intubation, feeding tube. He wanted everything! It was truly shocking that, despite years of unbearable pain, discomfort, and a multitude of health issues—heart problems, painful dialysis sessions, monthly drainage of his belly fluid, constant nausea, crippling joint pain, and unrelenting fatigue—he refused to give up. Even after all that suffering, he still wanted to explore every possible medical intervention available.

At this point, the path took a different turn. The doctors, who were just as shocked as I was, became more vocal and unhappy regarding their reluctance to provide care. The hospitalist told my father, in a tone that was more sarcastic than factual, that if he indeed wanted everything, or wanted to be full code, he would need to be transferred to another hospital. The doctors asked Dad if he was willing to be airlifted to that other hospital. My dad quickly replied, again without hesitation, "Of course. Why haven't you transferred me already?"

And just like that, the wheels were put in motion to request a transfer to a hospital that had the facilities and expertise to take care of my stubborn father. Amazingly, he was going to be transferred to the hospital I knew and trusted. That facility accepted, and the plan was set for transfer on Monday night. I was relieved that he'd finally communicated his wishes to the doctors and was getting the level of care he wanted.

Everything looked good, and I thought we'd beat death once again. Dad had overcome yet another medical crisis. But on my drive to the hospital to see him one last time before the transfer, the ICU called me. His nurse was speaking hurriedly and nearly breathlessly on the other end. She told me that a few minutes prior, his heart had stopped. They were in the midst of doing CPR. Dad was the one who'd decided he wanted to be full code, and he was getting the most aggressive care to try to save him. I started crying and telling her I was in the usual LA traffic and was doing my best to get there as fast as possible. Assuming Dad wouldn't survive this code and resuscitation, I thanked her for all she'd done for him.

I arrived at the hospital fifteen or twenty minutes later to find a group of doctors and nurses in my dad's room. The nurse ran out, excited to tell me they'd actually been successful in reviving Dad's heart and that he'd regained consciousness. As is common after CPR, he'd been intubated and had in his mouth a breathing tube connected to a machine. In a state of shock and joy, the nurse told me that after the intubation, Dad had regained complete alertness. When she had put cartoons on the TV, he'd frowned and motioned to her to change the channel. She told me, "I've never coded and done CPR on a patient who told me to change the channel ten minutes later."

After the cardiac arrest, he required more vasopressors added to the dizzying mix of medicines hanging from the poles in his room. As the doctors and nurses who'd worked on him started filing out of the room, I could see the concern on their faces. We all knew how this was going to end.

A day and a half later—in one of the most painful moments of my life—I had to make the decision to turn off and disconnect all the machines and medicines while Dad's eyes tracked my every move. He couldn't speak because there were tubes everywhere—in his mouth, nose, arms, neck, and legs. One connected him to the machine that was breathing for him, another fed him, another continuously dialyzed and filtered his blood, and many more bags of medicine kept his frail body a hair's breadth away from death. I held his hand and said my third goodbye of the week, very clear that this would be my final chance. There was no coming back from this.

The heartache and grieving process has continued in various forms since his passing. I can't help but replay his last week over and over in my mind, wishing it had been different. It's the pain and challenges I've experienced for years that made it so important for me to write this book. While my personal life has included a relentless stream of caregiving for sick relatives (and, therefore, many challenging hospital encounters), this particular end-of-life experience was the toughest.

I look back often, thinking of how I wished things had happened differently. In an ideal world, we would have been able to have some of these difficult conversations maybe a decade before they happened. I wish cultural norms hadn't made it disrespectful and improper to have frank conversations with my dad about his poor prognosis. I wish he'd understood the risks of CPR and ICU interventions. I wish that, whatever his beliefs and desires, he'd selected a healthcare proxy. I wish that, if he wasn't able to discuss these difficult topics with me or other family members, one of his many doctors had pulled him aside and asked him what he wanted. Of course, one of my main wishes is that he'd made different choices about where he chose to live. Dad's decision regarding his place of residence had everything to do with him being hospitalized in a medical center that didn't know anything about his medical history and prior care. Those decisions directly impacted us in that last week in a less-than-ideal way.

Ultimately, however, as I look back, I'm certain of one thing. I may not have had any control or say in where Dad chose to live or the hospital he was taken to. I may not have had control over (or agreed with) his decision to opt for the most aggressive care possible. I certainly would never have wanted to be in a position to make the decision to stop all lifesaving support. I am, however, certain that I did what I could to respect his wishes and advocate for him in every possible way until the last moment of his life. And that one fact brings me incredible peace and comfort.

As you navigate the complexities of healthcare, remember that you have numerous opportunities to advocate for yourself and your loved ones and regain control of your situation. By making informed decisions and being proactive, you can face challenges with confidence. You hold the power to chart your unique path through the healthcare system, and this book is here to support you every step of the way.

Love this book? Don't forget to leave a review!

Every review matters, and it matters a lot!

Head over to Amazon (or wherever you purchased this book) to leave an honest review for me.

I thank you endlessly.

NOTES

CHAPTER 1

[1] "Fast Facts on U.S. Hospitals, 2022: AHA," American Hospital Association, AHA.org, accessed August 11, 2023, https://www.aha.org/statistics/fast-facts-us-hospitals.

2 Sara Rosenbaum, David A. Kindig, Jie Bao, Maureen K. Byrnes, and Collin O'Laughlin, "The Value Of The Nonprofit Hospital Tax Exemption Was $24.6 Billion In 2011," *Health Affairs 34*, no. 7 (July 2015): 1225–1233, https://doi.org/10.1377/hlthaff.2014.1424.

3 "Revenue Ruling 56–185, 1956–1, C.B. 202, modified Rev. Rul. 69–545, 1969–2 C.B. 117," Internal Revenue Service, accessed September 30, 2017, https://www.irs.gov/pub/irs-tege/rr56-185.pdf.

4 Ge Bai, Hossein Zare, Matthew D. Eisenberg, Daniel Polsky, and Gerard F. Anderson, "Analysis Suggests Government And Nonprofit Hospitals' Charity Care Is Not Aligned With Their Favorable Tax Treatment," *Health Affairs 40*, no. 4 (April 2021): https://doi.org/10.1377/hlthaff.2020.01627.

5 Adam Andrzejewski, "Top U.S. 'Non-Profit' Hospitals & CEOS Are Racking up Huge Profits," Forbes, *Forbes Magazine*, June 26, 2019, https://www.forbes.com/sites/adamandrzejewski/2019/06/26/top-u-s-non-profit-hospitals-ceos-are-racking-up-huge-profits/?sh=3168e2e619df.

6 Samantha Liss, "Outlook for Nonprofit Hospitals Is 'Deteriorating,' Fitch Says," Healthcare Dive,

healthcaredive.com, August 17, 2022, https://www.healthcaredive.com/news/nonprofit-hospitals-outlook-deteriorating-fitch-ratings/629833/.

7   Melanie Evans, Max Rust, and Tom McGinty, "Big Nonprofit Hospitals Expand in Wealthier Areas, Shun Poorer Ones," *Wall Street Journal*, December 26, 2022, https://www.wsj.com/articles/nonprofit-hospitals-deals-tax-breaks-11672068264.

8   Bradford H. Gray, *For-Profit Enterprise in Health Care* (Washington, DC: The National Academies Press): 1986, https://doi.org/10.17226/653.

9   Karen Fisher, "Academic health centers save millions of lives," Association of American Medical Colleges, aamc.org, June 4, 2019, https://www.aamc.org/news/academic-health-centers-save-millions-lives#:~:text=In%20addition%2C%20major%20teaching%20hospitals,of%20all%20inpatient%20psychiatric%20beds.

10   Laura G. Burke et al., "Association Between Teaching Status and Mortality in US Hospitals," *JAMA 317*, no. 20 (2017): 2105–2113, https://jamanetwork.com/journals/jama/fullarticle/2627971.

11   James M. Hatten and Rose E. Connerton, "Urban and rural hospitals: How do they differ?" *Health Care Financial Review 8*, no. 2 (1986): 77–85, https://www.ncbi.nlm.nih.gov/pmc/articles/PMC4191541.

12   "1. The Importance of Rural Hospitals," Saving Rural Hospitals, ruralhospitals.chqpr.org, accessed November 16, 2023, https://ruralhospitals.chqpr.org/Importance.html#fnref9.

13   Hatten and Connerton, "Urban and rural hospitals: How do they differ?"

14   Peter Hutten-Czapski, "Rural-urban differences in emergency department wait times," *Canada Journal*

of Rural Medicine 15, no. 4 (2010): 153–155, PMID: 20875314.

15 "Rural Areas Have Fewer Health Care Providers" (infographic), NIHCM, updated October 20, 2020, https://nihcm.org/publications/rural-areas-have-fewer-health-care-providers.

16 "Rural Hospital Closures Threaten Access: Solutions to Preserve Care in Local Communities," American Hospital Association, AHA.org, accessed August 11, 2023, https://www.aha.org/2022-09-07-rural-hospital-closures-threaten-access.

17 Sally C. Curtin and Merianne Rose Spencer, "Trends in Death Rates in Urban and Rural Areas: United States, 2999–3029," National Center for Health Statistics, CDC.gov, accessed September 26, 2023, https://www.cdc.gov/nchs/products/databriefs/db417.htm.

18 John T. James, "A New, Evidence-Based Estimate of Patient Harms Associated with Hospital Care," *Journal of Patient Safety 9*, no. 3 (2013): 122–128, https://doi.org/10.1097/pts.0b013e3182948a69.

19 R. Monina Klevens et al., "Estimating health care-associated infections and deaths in U.S. hospitals, 2002," *Public Health Rep. 122*, no. 2 (2007): 160–166, https://doi.org/10.1177%2F003335490712200205.

20 "WHO launches first ever global report on infection prevention and control," World Health Organization, May 6, 2022, https://www.who.int/news/item/06-05-2022-who-launches-first-ever-global-report-on-infection-prevention-and-control#:~:text=On%20average%2C%201%20in%20every,newborns%20are%20particularly%20at%20risk.

CHAPTER 2

1   Bryan N. Batson and John M. Fitzpatrick, "Targeting Value-based Care with Physician-led Care Teams," *Journal Mississippi State Medical Association 63*, no. 1 (2022): 19–21.

2   "Scope of Practice: Education Matters," AMA, ama-assn.org, updated August 31, 2023, https://www.ama-assn.org/practice-management/scope-practice/scope-practice-education-matters.

3   Jennifer P. Stevens et al., "Comparison of Hospital Resource Use and Outcomes Among Hospitalists, Primary Care Physicians, and Other Generalists," *JAMA Internal Medicine 177*, no. 12 (2017): 1781–1787, https://doi.org/10.1001%2Fjamainternmed.2017.5824.

4   Yong-Fang Kuo and James S. Goodwin, "Effect of Hospitalists on Length of Stay in the Medicare Population: Variation According to Hospital and Patient Characteristics," *Journal of the American Geriatrics Society 58*, no. 9 (2010): 1649–1657, https://doi.org/10.1111/j.1532-5415.2010.03007.x.

CHAPTER 3

1   Kuldeep N. Yadav et al., "Approximately One in Three US Adults Completes Any Type of Advance Directive for End-of-Life Care," *Health Affairs (Project Hope) 36*, no. 7 (2017): 1244–1251, https://doi.org/10.1377/hlthaff.2017.0175.

2   Mary Jordan, "The retired pilot went to the hospital. Then his life went into a tailspin," *The Washington Post*, November 4, 2023, https://www.washingtonpost.com/nation/2023/11/04/florida-guardianship-investigation-safeguards/.

3   Lars W. Andersen et al., "In-Hospital Cardiac Arrest:
     A Review," *JAMA 321*, no. 12 (2019): 1200–1210,
     https://doi.org/10.1001/jama.2019.1696.
4   Abdul H. Qazi, Kevin Kennedy, Steven M. Bradley, Paul
     S. Chan, and American Heart Association Get With
     the Guidelines Resuscitation Investigators, "Impact
     of timing of cardiac arrest during hospitalization on
     survival outcomes and subsequent length of stay,"
     Resuscitation, no. 121 (2017): 117–122, https://doi.
     org/10.1016/j.resuscitation.2017.10.003.

CHAPTER 4

1   "Emergency Department Visits," National Center for
     Health Statistics, CDC.gov, accessed September 26,
     2023, https://www.cdc.gov/nchs/fastats/emergency-
     department.htm.
2   "The High Cost of Avoidable Hospital Emergency
     Department Visits," UnitedHealthGroup.com, July
     22,   2019,   https://www.unitedhealthgroup.com/
     newsroom/posts/2019-07-22-high-cost-emergency-
     department-visits.html.
3   Bart M. Demaerschalk et al., "Assessment of Clinician
     Diagnostic Concordance With Video Telemedicine
     in the Integrated Multispecialty Practice at Mayo
     Clinic During the Beginning of COVID-19 Pandemic
     From March to June 2020," *Health Informatics 5*,
     no. 9 (2022): e2229958, https://doi.org/10.1001/
     jamanetworkopen.2022.29958.
4   Casey Leins, "10 States With the Longest Emergency
     Room Waits," U.S. News, usnews.com, March 17,
     2020,   https://www.usnews.com/news/best-states/
     articles/2020-03-17/10-states-with-the-longest-
     emergency-room-wait-times; Clara Harter, "Long
     waits and hallway beds, as crowded ERs struggle to

meet patient demand," *Los Angeles Daily News*, May 8, 2023, https://www.dailynews.com/2023/05/08/long-waits-and-hallway-beds-as-crowded-ers-struggle-to-meet-patient-demand/.

5   M. C. Peterson, J. H. Holbrook, D. Von Hales, N. L. Smith, and L. V. Staker, "Contributions of the history, physical examination, and laboratory investigation in making medical diagnoses," *West J. Med. 156*, no. 2 (1992): 163–165, https://pubmed.ncbi.nlm.nih.gov/1536065/.

CHAPTER 5

1   Elazer R. Edelman and Mike Mussallem, "The pandemic has irreversibly changed America's health care system. Here's why we will all be feeling the consequences of delayed care for years to come," Fortune.com, February 21, 2023, https://fortune.com/2023/02/21/pandemic-irreversibly-changed-america-health-care-system-consequences-delayed-care-edelman-mussallem/.

2   "R3 Report I: Requirement, Rationale, Reference," issue 4, The Joint Commission, December 19, 2012, https://www.jointcommission.org/-/media/tjc/documents/ standards/r3-reports/r3_report_issue_4.pdf.

3   Zoubir Boudi et al., "Association between boarding in the emergency department and in-hospital mortality: a systematic review," *PLoS One 15*, no. 4 (2020): e0231253, https://doi.org/10.1371/journal.pone.0231253.

4   Kelly Mumford, "CRNA Independent Practice States," CCI Anesthesia, ccianesthesia.com, accessed October 30, 2023, https://www.ccianesthesia.com/crnas/crna-independent-practice-states; "Opt-Outs," ASA

Policy, American Society of Anesthesiologists, asahq. org, updated August 4, 2023, https://www.asahq. org/advocacy-and-asapac/advocacy-topics/opt-outs.

5   Mumford, "CRNA Independent Practice States"; "Opt-Outs."

6   Robert L. Kane, Tatyana A. Shamliyan, Christine Mueller, Sue Duval, and Timothy J. Wilt, "The association of registered nurse staffing levels and patient outcomes: systematic review and meta-analysis," *Medical Care 45*, no. 12 (2007): 1195–204, https://doi.org/10.1097/mlr.0b013e3181468ca3.

7   Junhyun Kim, Sungjae, Jinhee Park, and Eunhee Lee, "Multilevel factors influencing falls of patients in hospital: The impact of nurse staffing," *Journal of Nursing Management 27*, no. 5 (2019): 1011–1019, https://doi.org/10.1111/jonm.12765.

8   M. Di Muzio et al., "Can nurses' shift work jeopardize the patient safety? A systematic review," *European Review for Medical and Pharmacological Sciences 23*, no. 10 (2019): 4507–4519, https://doi.org/10.26355/eurrev_201905_17963.

9   Linda H. Aiken, Sean P. Clarke, Douglas M. Sloane, Julie Sochalski, and Jeffrey H. Silber, "Hospital nurse staffing and patient mortality, nurse burnout, and job dissatisfaction," *JAMA 288*, no. 16 (2002): 1987–1993, https://pubmed.ncbi.nlm.nih.gov/12387650/.

10   Robert G. Hill Jr., Lynn Marie Sears, and Scott W. Melanson, "4000 clicks: a productivity analysis of electronic medical records in a community hospital ED," *American Journal of Emergency Medicine 31*, no. 11 (2013): 1591–1594, https://doi.org/10.1016/j.ajem.2013.06.028.

11   Joshua W. Joseph et al., "Modelling attending physician productivity in the emergency department:

a multicentre study," *Emergency Medical Journal 35*, no. 5 (2018): 317–322, https://www.ncbi.nlm.nih.gov/pmc/articles/PMC5916102/.

12   Krisda H. Chaiyachati et al., "Assessment of inpatient time allocation among first-year internal medicine residents using time-motion observation," *JAMA Internal Medicine 179*, no. 6 (2019): 760–767, https://doi.org/10.1001/jamainternmed.2019.0095.

13   Margo Williams, "What's the benefit of patient, family engagement?" ACP Internist, April 2019, https://acpinternist.org/archives/2019/04/whats-the-benefit-of-patient-family-engagement.htm.

14   Daniel K. Brown, Jo L. Barton, and Valerie F. Gladwell, "Viewing nature scenes positively affects recovery of autonomic function following acute-mental stress," *Environmental Science and Technology 47*, no. 11 (2013): 5562–5569, https://doi.org/10.1021/es305019p.

CHAPTER 6

1   "Length of hospital stay" (indicator), OECD, oecd.org, 2023, accessed August 11, 2023, https://data.oecd.org/healthcare/length-of-hospital-stay.htm#indicator-chart.

2   Yogesh Moradiya, Santosh Murthy, Shreyansh Shah, and Sneha Modi, "Risk Factors And Outcomes of Prolonged Hospitalization After Intracerebral Hemorrhage in United States (P7.140)," *Neurology 82*, no. 10 (2014), https://n.neurology.org/content/82/10_Supplement/P7.140; Lauren Doctoroff and Shoshana J. Herzig, "Predicting Patients at Risk for Prolonged Hospital Stays," *Medical Care 58*, no. 9 (2020): 778–784, https://doi.org/10.1097%2FMLR.0000000000001345.

3   Emma Jane Zhao et al., "A long wait: barriers to discharge for long length of stay patients," *Postgraduate Medical Journal* 94, no. 1116 (2018): 546–550, https://doi.org/10.1136/postgradmedj-2018-135815.

4   Najma Siddiqi, Allan O. House, and John D. Holmes, "Occurrence and outcome of delirium in medical in-patients: a systematic literature review," *Age Ageing* 35, no. 4 (2006): 350–364, https://doi.org/10.1093/ageing/afl005.

5   Christina J. Hayhurst, Pratik P. Pandharipande, and Christopher G. Hughes, "Intensive Care Unit Delirium: A Review of Diagnosis, Prevention, and Treatment," *Anesthesiology 125*, no. 6 (2016): 1229–1241, https://doi.org/10.1097/ALN.0000000000001378.

6   Jin H. Han and Scott T. Wilber, "Altered Mental Status in Older Emergency Department Patients," Clinics in Geriatric Medicine 29, no. 1 (2013): 101–136, https://doi.org/10.1016/j.cger.2012.09.005.

7   Jane McCusker, Martin G. Cole, Nandini Dendukuri, and Eric Belzile, "Does delirium increase hospital stay?" *Journal of American Geriatric Society 51*, no. 11 (2003): 1539–46, https://doi.org/10.1046/j.1532-5415.2003.51509.x.

8   Jane McCusker, Martin Cole, Michal Abrahamowicz, Francois Primeau, and Eric Belzile, "Delirium predicts 12-month mortality," *Arch Intern Med. 162*, no. 4 (2002): 457–463, https://doi.org/10.1001/archinte.162.4.457.

9   Angela J. Gillis and Brenda MacDonald, "Unmasking delirium," *Canada Nurse 102*, no. 9 (2006): 18–24, PMID: 17168095.

10 R. S. Wilson, L. E. Hebert, P. A. Scherr, X. Dong, S. E. Leurgens, and D. A. Evans, "Cognitive decline after hospitalization in a community population of older

persons," *Neurology 78*, no. 13 (2012): https://doi.org/10.1212/WNL.0b013e31824d5894.

11 Ashley M. Campbell et al., "Melatonin for the prevention of postoperative delirium in older adults: a systematic review and meta-analysis," *BMC Geriatrics 19* (2019): 272, https://doi.org/10.1186%2Fs12877-019-1297-6.

12 Janey C. Mentes and Phyllis M. Gaspar, "Hydration Management," *Journal of Gerontology Nursing 46*, no. 2 (2020): 19–30, https://doi.org/10.3928/00989134-20200108-03.

13 Rita Rego, Daniela Barroso, and Elga Friere, "Prevalence of constipation on an internal medicine ward," *Aging Med (Milton) 6*, no. 1 (2023): 98–99, https://doi.org/10.1002%2Fagm2.12244.

14 Brigitta Fazzini et al., "The rate and assessment of muscle wasting during critical illness: a systematic review and meta-analysis," *Critical Care 27*, no. 2 (2023), https://doi.org/10.1186/s13054-022-04253-0.

15 Christine Boev and Elizabeth Kiss, "Hospital-Acquired Infections: Current Trends and Prevention," *Critical Care Nursing Clinics of North America 29*, no. 1 (2017): 51–65, https://doi.org/10.1016/j.cnc.2016.09.012.

16 "Methicillin-resistant *Staphylococcus aureus* (MRSA)," Healthcare Settings, Centers for Disease Control and Prevention, last reviewed February 28, 2019, https://www.cdc.gov/mrsa/healthcare/index.html.

17 "What is *C. diff*?" Centers for Disease Control and Prevention, cdc.gov, last reviewed September 7, 2022, https://www.cdc.gov/cdiff/what-is.html.

CHAPTER 7

1   Charlene Harrington, "Nursing Home Staffing Standards in State Statutes and Regulations," *UCSF Survey of Nursing Home Staffing Standards, 2007* (PDF), January 2008, https://www.justice.gov/sites/default/files/nursing_home_staffing_standards_in_state_statutes_and_regulations.pdf.

2   Susan D. Horn, Peter Buerhaus, Nancy Bergstrom, and Randall J. Smout, "RN staffing time and outcomes of long-stay nursing home residents: pressure ulcers and other adverse outcomes are less likely as RNs spend more time on direct patient care," *American Journal of Nursing 105*, no. 11 (2005): 58–70, https://doi.org/10.1097/00000446-200511000-00028; Lorraine J. Phillips, Nancy M. Birtley, Gregory F. Petroski, Carol Siem, and Marilyn Rantz, "An observational study of antipsychotic medication use among long-stay nursing home residents without qualifying diagnoses," *Journal of Psychiatry and Mental Health Nursing 25*, no. 8 (2018): 463–474, https://doi.org/10.1111/jpm.12488.

3   Charlene Harrington, John F. Schnelle, Margaret McGregor, and Sandra F. Simmons, "The need for higher minimum staffing standards in U.S. nursing homes," *Health Services Insights*, no. 9 (2016): 13–19, https://doi.org/10.4137%2FHSI.S38994.

4   Anil N. Makam et al., "The Clinical Course after Long-Term Acute Care Hospital Admission among Older Medicare Beneficiaries," *Journal of the American Geriatrics Society 67*, no. 11 (2019): 2282–2288, https://doi.org/10.1111/jgs.16106.

5   Mellanie V. Springer, Lesli E. Skolarus, Chunyang Feng, and James F. Burke, "Functional Impairment and Postacute Care Discharge Setting May Be Useful

for Stroke Survival Prognostication," *Journal of the American Heart Association 11*, no. 6 (2022): e024327, https://doi.org/10.1161%2FJAHA.121.024327.

CHAPTER 8

1   Hannah Wunsch et al., "ICU Occupancy and mechanical ventilator use in the United States," *Critical Care Medicine 41*, no. 12 (2013), https://doi.org/10.1097%2FCCM.0b013e318298a139.

2   Giacomo Bellani et al., "Epidemiology, Patterns of Care, and Mortality for Patients With Acute Respiratory Distress Syndrome in Intensive Care Units in 50 Countries," *JAMA 315*, no. 8 (2016): 788–800, https://doi.org/10.1001/jama.2016.0291.

3   "CPR Facts & Stats," American Heart Association, CPR.heart.org, accessed August 11, 2023, https://cpr.heart.org/en/resources/cpr-facts-and-stats.

4   Sagar Mallikethi-Reddy, "Incidence and Survival After In-Hospital Cardiopulmonary Resuscitation in Nonelderly Adults: US Experience, 2007 to 2012," *Circulation Cardiovascular Quality and Outcomes 10*, no. 2 (2017): e003194, https://doi.org/10.1161/circoutcomes.116.003194; William J. Ehlenbach et al., "The Epidemiology of In-Hospital Cardiopulmonary Resuscitation in Older Adults: 1992-2005," *New England Journal of Medicine 361*, no. 1 (July 2002): 22–31, https://doi.org/10.1056%2FNEJMoa0810245.

5   "Cognitive problems are common after cardiac arrest," Lund University, ScienceDaily, April 17, 2015, https://www.sciencedaily.com/releases/2015/04/150417085222.htm; "Cognitive problems are common after cardiac arrest," Lund University, April 17, 2015, https://www.lunduniversity.

lu.se/article/cognitive-problems-are-common-after-cardiac-arrest.

6   Eduard Kralj, Matej Podbregar, Nataša Nejžar, and Jože Balažic, "Frequency and number of resuscitation related rib and sternum fractures are higher than generally considered," *Resuscitation 93* (August 2015): 136–141, https://doi.org/10.1016/j.resuscitation.2015.02.034.

7   Kristin Schwab et al., "Trends in Endotracheal Intubation During In-Hospital Cardiac Arrests: 2001–2018," *Critical Care Medicine 50*, no. 1 (2022): 72–80, https://doi.org/10.1097/ccm.0000000000005120.

8   Reisfield et al., "Survival in cancer patients"; D. D. Tresch, J. M. Neahring, E. H. Duthie, D. H. Mark, S. K. Kartes, and T. P. Aufderheide, "Outcomes of cardiopulmonary resuscitation in nursing homes: can we predict who will benefit?" *American Journal of Medicine 95*, no. 2 (August 1993): 123–30, https://doi.org/10.1016/0002-9343(93)90252-k.

9   Kei Ouchi et al., "Prognosis After Emergency Department Intubation to Inform Shared Decision-Making," *Journal of American Geriatric Society 66*, no. 7 (2018): 1377–1381, https://doi.org/10.1111/jgs.15361.

10 Vincenzo Russotto et al., "Intubation Practices and Adverse Peri-intubation Events in Critically Ill Patients From 29 Countries," *JAMA 325*, no. 12 (2021): 1164–1172, https://doi.org/10.1001/jama.2021.1727.

11 Craig Kornbau, Kathryn C. Lee, Gwendolyn D. Hughes, and Michal S. Firstenberg, "Central line complications," *International Journal of Critical Illness and Injury Science 5*, no. 3 (2015): 170–178, https://doi.org/10.4103%2F2229-5151.164940.

12 Charalambos Charalambous et al., "Risk factors and clinical impact of central line infections in the

surgical intensive care unit," *Archives of Surgery 133*, no. 11 (1998): 1241–1246, https://doi.org/10.1001/archsurg.133.11.1241; "Variability of Surveillance Practices for Central Line–Associated Bloodstream Infections," The Joint Commission, jointcommission.org, accessed November 16, 2023, https://www.jointcommission.org/resources/patient-safety-topics/infection-prevention-and-control/central-line-associated-bloodstream-infections-toolkit-and-monograph/variability-of-surveillance-practices-for-central-lineassociated-bloodstream-infections-and-its-impl/#:~:text=Central%20line%2Dassociated%20bloodstream%20infections%20(CLABSIs)%20are%20health%20care,to%20%242.3%20billion%20a%20year.

13 Kornbau, Lee, Hughes, and Firstenberg, "Central line complications."

14 Kornbau, Lee, Hughes, and Firstenberg, "Central line complications."

15 Donald A. Brand et al., "Intensity of Vasopressor Therapy for Septic Shock and the Risk of In-Hospital Death," *Journal of Pain Symptom Management 53*, no. 5 (2017): 938–943, https://doi.org/10.1016/j.jpainsymman.2016.12.333.

16 Richard D. Fremont and Todd W. Rice, "How soon should we start interventional feeding in the ICU?" *Current Opinion in Gastroenterology 30*, no. 2 (2014): 178–181, https://doi.org/10.1097%2FMOG.0000000000000047.

17 Sunshine Barhorst, Richard M. Prior, and Daniel Kanter, "Implementation of a best-practice guideline: Early enteral nutrition in a neuroscience intensive care unit," *Journal of Parenteral and Enteral Nutrition 47*, no. 1 (2023): 87–91, https://doi.org/10.1002/jpen.2411.

18 Abdul Hasan Siddiqui et al., "Predictors of 15-Day Survival for the Intensive Care Unit Patient on Continuous Renal Replacement Therapy: A Retrospective Analysis," *Cureus 12*, no. 5 (2020): e8175, https://doi.org/10.7759/cureus.8175; Wouter De Corte et al., "Long-term outcome in ICU patients with acute kidney injury treated with renal replacement therapy: a prospective cohort study," *Critical Care 20*, no. 256 (2016), https://doi.org/10.1186/s13054-016-1409-z.

19 Siddiqui et al., "Predictors of 15-Day Survival."

20 Judy E. Davidson, Ramona O. Hopkins, Deborah Louis, and Theodore J. Iwashyna, "Post-intensive Care Syndrome," Society of Critical Care Medicine, sccm.org, 2013, https://www.sccm.org/MyICUCare/THRIVE/Post-intensive-Care-Syndrome; Anahita Rabiee et al., "Depressive symptoms after critical illness: a systematic review and meta-analysis," *Critical Care Medicine 44*, no. 9 (September 2016): 1744–1753, https://doi.org/10.1097%2FCCM.0000000000001811; George Zisopoulos, Pagona Roussi, and Eleni Mouloudi, "Psychological morbidity a year after treatment in intensive care unit," *Health Psychology Research 8*, no. 3 (December 2020): 8852, https://doi.org/10.4081%2Fhpr.2020.8852.

21 Cassiano Teixeira et al., "The Burden of Mental Illness Among Survivors of Critical Care—Risk Factors and Impact on Quality of Life: A Multicenter Prospective Cohort Study," *Chest Journal 160*, no. 1 (2021): 157–164, https://doi.org/10.1016/j.chest.2021.02.034.

22 Patricia Serrano et al., "Aging and Postintensive Care Syndrome—Family: A Critical Need for Geriatric Psychiatry," *American Journal of Geriatric Psychiatry*

27, no. 4 (2019): 446–454, https://doi.org/10.1016/j.jagp.2018.12.002.

23   Judy E. Davidson, Christina Jones, Joseph O. Bienvenu, "Family response to critical illness: Postintensive care syndrome–family," *Critical Care Medicine 40*, no. 2 (2012): 618–624, https://doi.org/10.1097/CCM.0b013e318236ebf9.

Made in the USA
Columbia, SC
12 October 2024

43498843R10104